My Dog Is Driving Me Crazy!

Diane Morgan

My Dog Is Driving Me Crazy!

Project Team
Editor: Stephanie Fornino
Copy Editor: Joann Woy
Indexer: Elizabeth Walker
Designer: Mary Ann Kahn

TFH Publications®
President/CEO: Glen S. Axelrod
Executive Vice President: Mark E. Johnson
Editor-in-Chief: Albert Connelly, Jr.
Production Manager: Kathy Bontz

TFH Publications, Inc.®
One TFH Plaza
Third and Union Avenues
Neptune City, NJ 07753

Printed and bound in China
14 15 16 17 18 19   1 3 5 7 9 8 6 4 2

Library of Congress Cataloging-in-Publication Data
Morgan, Diane, 1947-
  My dog is driving me crazy! : be smarter than your dog! : a practical
guide to understanding and correcting problem behaviors / Diane Morgan.
      p. cm.
  Includes index.
  ISBN 978-0-7938-0719-2 (alk. paper)
  1. Dogs--Behavior therapy. 2. Dogs--Behavior. 3. Dogs--Training. I.
Title.
  SF433.M66 2012
  636.7'0835--dc23
                          2012004515

This book has been published with the intent to provide accurate and authoritative information in regard to the subject matter within. While every reasonable precaution has been taken in preparation of this book, the author and publisher expressly disclaim responsibility for any errors, omissions, or adverse effects arising from the use or application of the information contained herein. The techniques and suggestions are used at the reader's discretion and are not to be considered a substitute for veterinary care. If you suspect a medical problem consult your veterinarian.

Note: In the interest of concise writing, "he" is used when referring to puppies and dogs unless the text is specifically referring to females or males. "She" is used when referring to people. However, the information contained herein is equally applicable to both sexes.

The Leader In Responsible Animal Care For Over 50 Years!®
www.tfh.com

Table of Contents

Introduction

> First the wolves were created. Then humans got hold of them and turned them into Chihuahuas, Beagles, and Nova Scotia Duck Tolling Retrievers. Now we have to live with them.
>
> —Diane Morgan

Dogs are intelligent animals, which may explain why they're so good at outwitting their humans!

This is a book about "problem behaviors" in dogs. A problem behavior can be defined as conduct of which people don't approve. It is something that interferes with our comfort and convenience. However, things like barking, digging, biting, stealing food, jumping up, and running off are normal canine behaviors, not moral failings. Dogs are imprinted with the compulsion to do all these things; extra-smart dogs can even invent novel ways to torture their humans (like hiding their glasses or urinating on their homework). From the canine side of the fence, it's people who exhibit "problem behaviors" by tying them up, putting them in cages, kicking them off the couch, and controlling their diet. Dogs are simply trying to get along in the world without working too hard or losing too much sleep. The fact that they have managed to get away with all this for so long and made us foot the bills is just an example of how deviously bright they really are.

Dogs are smart—there's no doubt about it. Early on, they surmised which way the winds of evolution were blowing and became the first species to join forces with human beings. How has this remarkable state of affairs come to pass? It's still pretty much a mystery. On some long ago day or night (date and location still hotly debated), the wolf-that-became-a-dog made a strange bargain, one never made before or since by any predator: to link his fate with ours. Over millennia, dogs have exchanged a precarious existence of cold weather and uncertain diet for an indoor lifestyle with a cozy bed, central heating, ample food, and regular health care.

Together, we humans and our dogs have hunted, scavenged, and scrounged our way across the face of the earth. Wherever we are, dogs are, even though neither species has kept strictly to the terms of the agreement we made. Humans have abused dogs, neglected them, and genetically contorted them into them into unnatural sizes, shapes, and hair styles. No wolf ever asked to be a Toy Poodle or lumbering Bulldog. And as for dogs....well, that's what this book is all about.

The Truth About Problem Behaviors

Dogs were not always freeloaders. In their early years, they worked for their keep by learning a trade: They became sled pullers, hunters, sheepherders, or guard dogs. Eventually, however, some of them discovered that they could turn themselves into little puffs of fur and "cute" their way into the human heart. Soon, even huskies and mastiffs and retrievers caught on; today, more than 90 percent of dogs do absolutely nothing to earn a living except hang around and look like they're paying attention.

But here's the rub. The same traits that we prized in working dogs and that are necessary to life as a wolf (nipping, vocalizing, barking, digging, chasing, and fighting, for example) were

Your dog responds to the conditions that you provide and the expectations that you communicate.

labeled nuisance behavior in pets, even though they are completely natural. We are annoyed when our Shelties bark, our Huskies run off, and our hounds ignore our desperate shouted commands. But all of this is part of a behavior package inserted into their genetic structure. We actually bred these dogs to have just these traits—and complained about them later, blaming and punishing dogs for simply being the creatures we made them. All of us are victims of our own civilization.

And civilization is not very civilized for dogs or humans. Too often, it's noisy, crowded, boring, violent, and polluted. Dogs were meant to run free, follow us everywhere, roll in carrion, attack strangers, and bay at the moon. Now, we want them to stay alone all day, be nice to strangers, smell nice, and keep quiet. We are asking our pets to be "unnatural" for most of their lives.

However, the situation is not hopeless. Solving a problem behavior starts by learning. Therefore, if you want to change your dog's bad behavior, you'll need to change your own. Your dog responds to the conditions that you provide and the expectations that you communicate. Dogs are smart, but their behavior is not as malleable as ours, and they are more powerfully controlled by instinct.

Because dogs are "our" creatures, we are legally and ethically responsible for their welfare and behavior. This book will help you do that. It will show you how to listen to your dog and figure out why he doing what he is doing. Understanding is the beginning of wisdom. It takes a wise person to train a dog.

How to Use This Book

This book is set up in a clear, easy-to-use manner to make tackling problem behaviors as hassle-free as possible.

Part I

Part I will give you a brief history of our history with the canine species and an introduction to the basic principles and mysteries of dog training.

Part II

In Part II, we get down to specifics. Every chapter deal with a specific problem, its cause, and some suggestions for dealing with it.

The Problem

As mentioned, problem behavior is simply conduct of which we don't approve—chasing, barking, digging, or whatever. In many cases, it's perfectly "natural." When it's not, it's often a response to what the dog perceives as *your* problem behavior. For example, a dog may exhibit separation anxiety when left alone for long periods. In frustration and anxiety, he tears up the house. That's the problem—for you. But for him, the problem is that *you* have unaccountably gone off and left him alone.

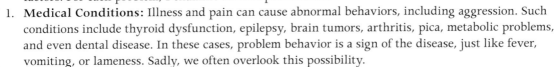

Because dogs evolved from wolves, much of their behavior is shaped by this ancient heritage.

The Cause

Problem behaviors can be caused by different variables, including medical conditions, wolf heritage, breed predilection and genetics, and environmental factors. For each problem, I examine all four possibilities.

1. **Medical Conditions:** Illness and pain can cause abnormal behaviors, including aggression. Such conditions include thyroid dysfunction, epilepsy, brain tumors, arthritis, pica, metabolic problems, and even dental disease. In these cases, problem behavior is a sign of the disease, just like fever, vomiting, or lameness. Sadly, we often overlook this possibility.

2. **Wolf Heritage:** Because dogs evolved from wolves, much of their behavior is shaped by this ancient heritage. Almost all of a dog's natural "problem" behaviors hark back to lupine origins: chasing, vocalizing, aggression, digging, and so forth. However, it's important to remember that in other ways dogs have evolved behaviorally away from wolves, which is why they make good pets. Learning how wolves behave gives us good clues—not complete answers—as to the origins of some dog behaviors. Keep in mind, though, that we actually don't know a heck of a lot about wolf behavior. Most of the studies have been done on captive packs and packs in which there is a considerable mixture of dog and coyote genes. And some of what we thought we knew has turned out to be false.

3. **Breed Predilection and Genetics:** Breed predilection includes behaviors that have been selected for in specific breeds. It takes into account both conformational and dispositional/ behavioral factors. A team of Basset Hounds will never win the Iditarod, for example, because

they are neither temperamentally disposed nor physically suited to the task. And there's something else to consider: Working dogs and pet dogs of the same breed, while they may look rather alike, often have few behavioral characteristics in common. A dog bred to have the true working characteristics of his breed generally makes a poor pet. For example, Border Collies are justly famous for their sheep-controlling "eye." This stare is inborn and genetically transferred in the breed and cannot be trained into a dog. In fact, real training cannot begin until the dog actually "shows eye," as they say in the sheepherding business. However, the famous eye is possessed only in real, working Border Collies. The trait is winnowed out in pet dogs because it is connected with too much "undesirable" stalking behavior in family dogs. Dogs from show lines may also be undesirable as pets.

When dog breeding began, breeders bred dogs to do a job—they didn't care about looks. They cared about results and had no fear of cross-breeding whenever they felt it might improve the working abilities of their dogs. Some of the most recognizable features of a particular breed are merely by-products (genetic tagalongs) of the skills the breeder was looking for. But with today's pet and show market focused almost totally on outward appearance, cross-breeding is not permitted and the results are often handsome, exaggerated, showy creatures who can do none of the things they were designed for—and who also frequently lack the gentle temperament most people want in a pet. Even the physical characteristics that breeders *want* in a dog have become so exaggerated they are often unhealthy. We have Bassets who trip over their own ears, Bulldogs with muzzles so short they can't breathe correctly, and toy dogs with mouths so small their teeth won't grow in properly. The situation in some breeds is *so* bad that the dogs cannot mate or give birth naturally anymore. It's a sad state of affairs, but it's true.

4. **Environmental Factors:** Environment shapes behavior. In this section we'll consider which specific elements in a dog's home or background may have led to a certain challenging behavior.

We have to remember, however, that every dog is genetically limited in exactly how much the environment can shape behavior. For example, no matter how gifted a teacher you may be, you can't teach your dog to read and write. In the same way, you can't teach a Corgi to point and hunt pheasant or an Irish Setter to be a disciplined and effective guard dog. Environment works to shape behavior, not to create it.

Sidebar #3:
WHEN ALL ELSE FAILS

Here are listed some "last-ditch" efforts that may pay off when other, usually simpler and more reliable methods, have failed to work.

What to Do

Here I offer some possible solutions and various tactics. Not all training or management techniques work for all dogs (or for people either). That's why, in each section, I've provided a number of *different* strategies for you to experiment with. Sometimes the solutions appear conflicting; that's because they are. Every dog is an individual, and a solution that works well for one dog may actually increase undesirable behavior in another. I've started with the most basic and widely applicable tactics, then proceeded to the more difficult, expensive, and in some cases, "iffy" solutions.

What Not to Do

Each section concludes with "What Not to Do." Many of our first impulses to correct a bothersome behavior are counterproductive. Avoid them.

Sidebar #4:
TRAINING CHECKLIST

✓ This sidebar summarizes the main training points of the chapter in checklist form.

Part I
Why Dogs Do What They Do

Chapter 1

Our Relationship With Dogs

Throughout history, humans and dogs have had a complex relationship. Scientifically, a relationship that benefits both species is called mutualism. In the case of dogs and people, we feed them and love them, and in return they provide us with emotional support, hunting and herding assistance, and more. But it's always been more complicated than that. At various times in our history, dogs have been our rivals, our enemies, our victims, our property, and our best friends. They capture criminals, locate lost people, and sniff out bombs, tumors, bedbugs, and drugs. They befriend folks in nursing homes, allow blind people to become more independent, and help kids learn to read. There are hundreds of instances every year in which a selfless hero dog saves a human life, often at the cost of his own.

Humans and their dogs enjoy a relationship called "mutualism," one that benefits both species.

Not that it always works out that way, of course. In reality, you're more likely to be bitten by a dog than rescued by one. In the United States, every day, about 1,000 people are treated in emergency rooms for dog bites. Most of the victims are children, half of whom are bitten in the face. Dog bite losses exceed $1 billion per year, with over $300 million paid by homeowners' insurance. And in 2010, there were 34 fatal dog attacks. But people seem to be more afraid of sharks and falling meteors. Resourceful as they are, killer dogs have gone far beyond the old-fashioned bite in their efforts to get rid of us. Dogs take advantage of modern technology. In 2008, a three-year-old yellow Labrador Retriever in Oregon shot his owner in the leg with a shotgun while they were out duck hunting. He also put a few holes in the boat. A Great Dane in Memphis shot his owner in the back by knocking a pistol off a coffee table and causing it to discharge. Dogs were also blamed on two different occasions (one in Florida and one in California) by husbands who declared that the household pet somehow managed to acquire a handgun and kill their wives.

Nor do dogs stop at firearms violations. Vehicular attempted homicide is becoming a favored modus operandi. Every once in a while, for example, dogs get behind the wheel of a car and somehow manage to shift from neutral into drive (presumably by accident, but you never know) and terrorize the neighborhood. In 2010, a Florida man was checking under the hood of his 5,000-pound (2,268-kg) Ford F-150 truck, which was parked in neutral with the engine on, when his Bulldog Killys jumped in and knocked it into gear. The truck started moving and ran over his owner, fortunately without producing life-threatening injuries. In 2008, a 70-pound (32-kg) pit bull in Oklahoma managed to drive his owner's car away from a car wash while the man was diligently scrubbing the hood. In 2007, a black Labrador Retriever named Charlie drove his owner's car into a river. It's not just in the United States, either. A New Zealand dog drove the family car through a cafe window. Nor do dogs confine their deadly efforts to autos. In September 2010, a Florida man named James Land was pitched out of his boat. While he clung patiently to a buoy waiting for help, his enterprising fellow passenger, a Jack Russell Terrier named Lucy, drove off with the boat to Pompano Beach and made a safe landing. Land was forced to swim a mile (1.5 km) back to shore. He claimed to be delighted to be reunited with the dog who heartlessly abandoned him to the waves.

More disturbingly, according to the National Fire Protection Association, dogs accidentally start about 1,000 house fires every year—knocking over candles and the like. In 2009, a dog named Alfie turned on the griddle attachment to the stove and toasted the entire kitchen. Alfie was sorry afterward.

Scientists have confirmed that dogs experience a wide range of "human" feelings.

How Smart Are Dogs?

So just how smart is the dog? Stanley Coren, Professor Emeritus of Psychology at the University of British Columbia, who researches both human and animal behaviors (and is the author of *The Intelligence of Dogs*), points to studies that adapt skills tests designed for young children to dogs. They reveal that our furry friends are about as smart as a two-year-old child and can learn about 165 words, signs, and signals. Smarter dogs can learn much more. In fact, some researchers are teaching guide dogs to recognize simple words by sight—actual reading. Others, at least according to their trainers, can do basic addition and subtraction. "You're not going to want your dog to be your accountant and do your taxes," Coren said, "but it's a useful skill." In addition, dogs who are actively worked—that is, given jobs to do and problems to solve—grow new connections in their brains and systematically become even more intelligent.

Dogs are not simply intellectually smart, however. They are also emotional, which requires a separate but equally important kind of intelligence. Scientists now acknowledge what dog lovers have always known: Dogs experience a wide range of "human" feelings: love, jealousy, pride, pique, boredom, and worry.

Even their outlook on life seems as variable as their owners'. Michael Mendl, head of the Animal Welfare and Behavior research group at Bristol University's School of Clinical Veterinary Science, headed a 2010 project in which 24 male and female dogs of different ages were tested for, of all things, optimism. In the first test, each dog was taken to a room where a researcher interacted positively with him for 20 minutes. The next day, the researcher did the same thing but left after only five minutes. Some dogs happily awaited the person's return, while others barked and

Sociability and Intelligence

The August 16, 2010, issue of *Time* magazine listed social carnivores like dogs as "sort of smart"—smarter than bison but dumber than crows. And indeed, it turns out that sociability and intelligence are connected. A study, published in the *Proceedings of the National Academy of Sciences* and led by Dr. Susanne Shultz of Oxford University, examined the evolution of the brain in different groups of mammals. The results showed that the more social an animal is, the larger the brain. This is the suggested reason why dogs outrank cats on nearly every intelligence scale devised. But cat owners shouldn't despair. Studies also show that cat owners are smarter (or at least more educated) than dog owners. Dr. Shultz told the *Telegraph*: "Dogs have always been regarded as the more social animals, while cats like to get on with their own thing alone. But it appears that interaction is good for the brain and extends to other species, like ourselves."

became anxious. Anxious dogs were labeled pessimists. Next, the researchers trained the dogs to understand that a bowl on one side of a room was full of delicious food, while a bowl on the other side was empty. The researchers then placed bowls at ambiguous places and observed how quickly the dogs would go to the bowls. "Dogs who ran fast to these ambiguous locations, as if expecting the positive food reward, were classed as making relatively optimistic decisions," announced Mendl. "Interestingly, these dogs tended to be the ones who also showed the least anxiety-like behavior when left alone for a short time." I leave it to the reader to determine the scientific value of these studies.

Our Emotional Connection

Despite our occasional difficulties with the canine species (which, after all, are molehills compared to the mountains of grief our fellow human beings cause us), dogs remain our best friends, playmates, therapists, and buffers against loneliness and sorrow. They are more important to our lives than ever, no longer as employees or servants but as friends and family. And the farther we humans get from nature and the farther dogs get from wolves, the closer we get to each other.

A 2010 survey conducted by Kelton Research, a marketing research company, found that 74 percent of the 1,001 dog owners polled believe that their dog's body language or facial expressions let them know how their pet is feeling. Seventy percent said that they have "shared a look" with their dog on at least one occasion. Nearly half reported that they know what their

Despite our occasional difficulties with the canine species, they remain our best friends and playmates.

Even though they are domesticated, every single dog on earth carries his inherent wildness deep within.

pet is thinking, and more than a third said that they've had an entire "conversation" with their dogs without saying anything at all. And almost 90 percent reported that their dogs knew when their owners had had a bad day and tried to comfort them. Two-thirds claimed that their dogs were more dependable than their human friends, and almost three-quarters of the respondents claimed that they would rather take a walk with their dog when they were upset than with a person. Heady stuff.

Our connection with dogs runs deep, in sickness as well as in health. Dogs and people get many of the same ailments, both physical and mental: diabetes, epilepsy, Cushing's and Addison's disease, obesity, obsessive-compulsive disorders, allergies, heart problems, arthritis, depression, and cancer. In fact, according to Andy Clark, professor of biology at Pennsylvania State University, "If you compare human diseases with their dog equivalents, you find that for over 350 diseases the dog equivalent is precisely the same disease that humans get."

And there's more. A study published in the July 2010 *Proceedings of the Royal Society* in the United Kingdom indicates that dogs imitate their owners' movements and behaviors even when it appears that they have no reason to do so. "This suggests that, like humans, dogs are subject to 'automatic imitation'; they cannot inhibit . . . the tendency to imitate head use and/or paw use," concluded University of Vienna researcher Friederike Range, the study's lead author. "This finding suggests that the dogs brought with them to the experiment a tendency automatically to imitate hand use and/or paw use by their owner; to imitate these actions even when it was costly to do so." All too human, the dog is of our tribe now.

The Wildness Within

And yet. There remains something in every dog—deep down, some shadowed memory, some flicker in the blood—that whispers old secrets and reminds even the most frou-frou among them that he is somehow still more than a dog. He must remember, at some inconceivably primitive level, the run and the hunt and the fight and the passion—all that wild old life under the ferocious twinkle of a fading star.

Those days are gone. But the spirit that made that ancient, dangerous, and romantic existence possible still surges in the heart of every dog, including yours. Every single dog on earth carries the wildness deep within. Indeed, most taxonomists list dogs as a subspecies of their ancestors. Wolves are *Canis lupis*, while dogs are *Canis lupus familiaris*: the familiar wolf, or even more cozily, the family wolf—emphasis on "wolf." However, no longer do dogs and wolves recognize each other as brothers. They avoid each other whenever possible, and unavoidable contacts are likely to be unpleasant. The spiritual divide is vast although not complete. Genetically, dogs and wolves are still very, very close; they can and occasionally do interbreed.

And it's from the big-brained wolf that dogs get their smarts. The flexible intelligence that allowed wolves to live on every continent, in every climate, thrives in your dog. The wolf who scavenged when he could not kill and ate berries when the scavenging got thin has become the dog who eats lamb and rice, blueberry pancakes, leftover spaghetti, and dried-up stuff called "kibble" that might be made of anything.

Your dog shares most of your world, but his kingdom is not quite yours. Genetically close to a wolf, culturally much closer to humans, the dog occupies a twilight kingdom, a Bardo zone between the pack and the parlor, between caribou and chicken nuggets. Physically, too, they are a fluid species: They can be Mastiffs and Maltese, Afghans and Affenpinschers.

STRENGTH IN NUMBERS

Dogs are so successful (thanks to us) that they now outnumber wolves by 1,000 to 1. Right now there are about 400,000,000 dogs on the planet.

As highly social animals, dogs are both cooperative and competitive.

And while his world shares many features of our own, it's still very different. The Universe of Dog is dimmer by day and brighter by night than ours. It is enriched with odors we can't smell and sounds we can't hear. It has, perhaps, weird vibrations and mysterious auras. We can't partake of it completely. In many respects, dogs and people live in a parallel universe. So how do we communicate? Simple. It's magic.

Yes, dogs are magical creatures. They are the true werewolves of the earth: part wild beast, part highly civilized *bon vivants*. A Borzoi can run down and kill his lupine cousin in the morning and cuddle up and gently lick a child's face by evening.

However, most of today's clever and conniving canines are no longer especially interested in running down caribou, savaging strangers, and sleeping outside in a blizzard. They have bigger fish to fry: their owners. Using age-old lupine techniques, our pets stalk us, much as they hunted the ancient caribou—watching and waiting for one mistake. One slip in our attention or control, one moment of softness, and the steak or soft spot on the couch is theirs. In other words, dogs capitalize on our mental slowness and emotional weaknesses. They've taken the ancestral skills that made them such superb predators and transformed them into tools for modern living. Dogs are social, observant, opportunistic problem solvers. As highly social animals, dogs are both cooperative and competitive. (Loner animals like housecats are not much of either.)

And to make the most out of family living, dogs are tireless observers—they know you a lot better than you know them. They spend most of their day carefully studying you, at least when they are not snoozing. Even then, they are often not quite as asleep as you may think and spend more time analyzing your face, voice, and gestures than you may imagine.

From their careful observations flows their problem-solving expertise. This is mainly expressed by exploiting their "owners" to achieve their objectives and to learn quickly how much they can get away with. This is usually quite a bit, because frankly, most humans aren't quite smart enough to outwit them. But *you* can, if only you take a fraction of the time studying him as he does you. We are, after all, the superior species. Right? This book will show you how to prove this daring hypothesis: You can indeed be smarter than your dog.

Chapter 2

Wolves:
Where the Problems Began

Everything you see in your pet dog originated in the wild blood of the wolf. The particular wolf species responsible is the gray wolf. Dogs have no other ancestors. Every one of them, from the Maltese to the Mastiff, has an equal share in the lupine heritage, even though you wouldn't know it to look at them.

The Origin of the Dog

The mystery of domestication is slowly unraveling, and scientists now think it was initiated by wolves and not us. In other words, early humans didn't kidnap a wolf cub and raise it as their own, as we used to believe. (Even if you raise a wolf cub like a dog, it still grows up to be uncomfortably wolfish in behavior.) It appears that certain wolves, perhaps submissive types who were less successful hunters but who had devolved some social skills to make up for it, started hanging around campfires and scavenging from people rather than their own kind. The wild populations slowly began to separate into the hunters and the scavengers.

The latter, because of their steadier although probably poorer diet, multiplied quickly and remained smaller, consuming fewer (but infinitely safer) calories. They could do away with the big teeth and the big frightening heads that supported them. (Domestic dogs, even giant breeds like Great Danes, have much smaller teeth than wolves do. That's probably for the best.) The details will always be murky, but the results are stunningly clear: Wolves turned themselves into dogs, and humans turned dogs into Chihuahuas, Poodles, and Chesapeake Bay Retrievers.

Ancient Breeds

The most truly ancient breeds of dogs were sighthounds and sled dogs. Later came sheepdogs (both guardians and herders) and hunting types. Many lapdogs, too, are of ancient lineage. From a genetic point of view, there are just five major dog groups: 1. ancient and Asian dogs; 2. hunting and gundogs; 3. mastiffs and terriers; 4. herding dogs and sighthounds; and 5. mountain dogs. Where this leaves the Affenpinscher is hard to say.

Only a couple of years ago, scientists were pretty sure that wolves turned into dogs in the Middle East; however, the very latest findings trace canine origins to southern East Asia. A study released November 23, 2011, suggests that the region south of the Yangtze River was the

No matter your breed's size or shape, all dogs have a common ancestor: the wolf.

principal (and probably) only birthplace of dogs. According to Dr. Peter Savolainen, a top evolutionary geneticist, earlier studies overlooked Y-chromosomal DNA from this region. According to his study, which analyzed gene samples from male dogs all over the world, about half of the gene pool was universally shared everywhere in the world, but the dogs from the south China region contained the entire range of genetic diversity, proving that the gene pool everywhere else most likely originated there. Stay tuned; the argument isn't over. The proponents of a Middle Eastern origin have archaeological data to back them up.

Unlike wolves, dogs are easily domesticated and make wonderful family companions.

What we do know is that even back then, we didn't just "have" dogs. We loved them. One ancient burial site revealed a woman with a puppy curled up in her arms. (The oldest remains discovered so far of a true dog were dug up in Switzerland and estimated to be about 14,000 years old.)

For the love bond to be successful, however, changes had to be made. For all their many virtues, wolves don't make good pets. We keep dogs rather than wolves because dogs can stand the thought of living with us and wolves can't. Wolves don't domesticate and won't learn tricks. While you've probably seen trained lions, tigers, apes, bears, sea lions, fleas, and elephants, you've never seen a trained wolf. Even wolves brought up in the house like puppies never learn to "read your face" the way dogs do. They can never acquiesce to walking politely on a leash, and they can't be housetrained. They don't sit, lie down, or come reliably when called. They will also, unpredictably and in their own good time, attack their "owners." Nor can you pat even a human-socialized wolf the way you might give your dog a hearty pat. Wolves interpret such petting as aggressive and will bite in response.

Even partial successes along this line often end up as disasters. The noted cynologist (that's fancy talk for "dog expert" with academic credentials) Erik Zimen worked intensively with some zoo-born, hand-raised

Fun Fact

The domestic dog is the only member of the canine family (Canidae) to be fully domesticated, although the red fox (*Vulpes vulpes*) and the raccoon dog (*Nyctereutes procyonides*) have been kept in captivity for generations for their fur.

WOLVES	DOGS
find and devour their own natural food in an ecologically sound manner	eat chemically enhanced kibble
self-groom	require brushes, combs, shampoos, detanglers, ear cleaners, toenail trimmers, their own toothbrushes and toothpaste, and regular trips to the boutique
live outside and like it	prefer room temperature housing, comfortable heated beds, and raincoats in inclement weather
largely free of genetic diseases	subject to more than 200 genetic diseases, plus "civilized" ailments like heart disease, obesity, arthritis, cancer, and other products of modern life
free of psychological ailments	prey to separation anxiety, obsessive-compulsive behaviors, untargeted aggression, and depression
mate for life	cat around every chance they get...pardon the pun

wolves and actually got them to pull a sled. Sort of. They ignored the musher's directions and went in whatever direction they felt like. When one of them got tired, he would lie down and to heck with the rest of the team. Occasionally, the whole pack of them would get into a terrific fight with each other over perceived territorial violations, and the entire team would have to be unhooked at peril to life and limb.

The chart above presents a basic comparison of dogs and wolves.

So Why Do We Keep Them?

As you probably know by now, dogs come with a multitude of challenges. Despite the centuries of lounging by the fire, despite both careful breeding and random acts of love, they have retained a great deal of their original unpleasant behavior. They howl. They dig. They beg. They bite. They escape. They chase. And as mentioned previously, they have now learned to set fires, shoot their owners, and abscond with the family car or boat.

But there's more. Dogs are expensive to care for, time consuming, messy, and noisy. In fact,

Dr. Nicholas Dodman, an animal-behavior specialist at Tufts University, estimates that at least 40 percent of the 77.5 million dogs in the United States have some kind of behavioral disorder. They can also transmit diseases like cryptosporidiosis, giardiasis, leptospirosis, rabies, scabies, ringworm, roundworm, and methicillin-resistant *Staphylococcus aureus* (MRSA) to their owners. Still, we can't seem to live without them.

Because few of us need dogs these days for hunting or sheepherding, why do we bother with them? The answer is frighteningly simple: We keep dogs because they are the only creatures in the universe other than a few (very few) of our own species who truly love us. Dogs are flexible and undemanding. They will put up with eating the dreck called kibble because their owners are too lazy to take them out hunting for game and too cheap to buy them a steak. They cheerfully consent to wearing a collar and being led about on a leash. They will sit, beg, and play dead on command. They allow themselves to be given ridiculous haircuts and have their ears cleaned, teeth brushed, and toenails clipped.

Dogs are easy to get along with in other ways too. Pragmatic to the core, they don't seem to notice (or at least make no inquires or judgments about) their owner's race, sexual orientation, criminal record, ethnic heritage, gender, religion, weight, hairstyle, lifestyle, salary, age, or political affiliation. They are always happy to see us and don't complain what a terrible day they've had. A dog will never ask you for your green card or demand to know if you have any pre-existing medical conditions.

Dogs are sociable animals who are easy to get along with and love spending time with their humans.

He'll never ask for a raise or want to have the bathroom remodeled. Any human competent enough to get dinner on the floor at a reasonable hour and who has a couch is good enough. If they hand out treats or belly rubs, so much the better.

We have dogs because we love them and they love us. Now why can't we all just get along?

Chapter 3

And Then We Started Breeding Them

While the basic domestication process of dogs has been pretty much complete for a few thousand years, we can't seem to stop tinkering with them. We weren't completely satisfied with our original wolf-dogs and their wolfish behavior, which may have included occasional bouts of dietary indiscretion (meaning the "pets" devoured their "owners").

Humans decided to make their new pets more user-friendly, and in the process, discovered selective breeding. We learned that dogs could be induced to morph into various sizes, colors, and hair types, and develop skill sets that wolves never thought about. Indeed, it's safe to say that dogs are the most diverse species on earth. If human beings were as variable in looks and size as dogs, some of us would be 22 feet (6.5 m) tall and weigh more than 1,000 pounds (453.5 kg).

How Dogs Diversified

How did this come about? After all, wolves all look and act pretty much alike. So how does it happen that dog breeds are so different from each other? The secret is apparently in the weirdness of dog/wolf genetic structure. In human beings (and agricultural plants), for instance, most physical characteristics are powered by clusters of genes, each of which contributes only a small part to the total effect. In dogs, though, things are different. For the most part, very specific genes account for specific physical traits, and these few genes can be shifted around to create an amazing diversity.

For example, short-legged dogs (and there are at least 19 such breeds, including Dachshunds, Corgis, and Basset Hounds) depend upon a single mutant gene, called a retrogene, to account for their dwarfish appearance. In this case, it's an extra copy of a gene that controls a growth-promoting protein called FGF4 (fibroblast growth factor). The retrogene causes an overproduction of the FGF4 protein, which scientists believe may trigger key growth receptors at the wrong

Dogs are the most diverse species on earth.

stages of fetal development. In addition, smaller breeds like Dachshunds, Beagles, Jack Russell Terriers, and Brittanys have a mutant form of another gene, the IGF1 gene, which controls body size. Wolves and larger dogs do not have this variant of the IGF1 gene; this indicates that the mutation for small size emerged *after* dogs were domesticated. But it must have occurred very early because all small dog breeds have some version of the gene. Subsequent studies identified genes controlling leg width, skull shape, ear position, and back arch.

Genes account for the variations in different dog breeds, such as the skin wrinkling found in the Chinese Shar-Pei.

The same is basically true for the genes that control fur types, skin wrinkling, coat patterns, and colors. Coat color (along with size), in fact, may have been one of the earliest results of human breeding efforts—but not on purpose. There is some evidence that, at least early on, coat color was associated with temperament. And a docile temperament was of primary importance to the first dog breeders. Research suggests that small, pale-coated dogs were easiest to manage; the earliest dogs, like the modern Dingo and New Guinea Singing Dog, were tawny yellow.

The main point is that by manipulating just a handful of genes, we can produce a vast multitude of dog breeds. By saying that dog genes have to be manipulated, I don't mean that the early dog breeders went messing around in laboratories. But they did keep a sharp eye out for individuals with traits they wanted and encouraged or forced dogs who shared those traits to mate. From such a process emerged the first herding, sledding, hunting, and guarding dogs.

Thus, over the centuries, we have distilled the complex stew of doggy genes into separate, identifiable breeds; that great generalist, the wolf, morphed into many highly specialized dog breeds. While no domestic dog has all the skills that could enable him to live in the wild, many breeds have developed unique abilities that far surpass those of their ancestors. Greyhounds can outrun a wolf, and Bloodhounds can follow an ice-cold trail better than any wolf. (It is not in a wolf's interest to follow a cold trail.) Border Collies have honed a wolf's inherent herding abilities down to a precise science. Sled dogs were bred to have weaker "hierarchical behavior" so that their handlers could switch them from one position to another without a fight breaking out, as happened with Zimen's sled wolves. (See Chapter 2).

Why Breeding Matters

So while it is not the sole determinant of behavior, breeding matters. Dog breeds were not developed only (or even in many cases mainly) to look a certain way but to do certain jobs and thus behave in certain ways. Although each dog is an individual, there are definite tendencies that flow along breed lines. Dogs bred to be guardians are by nature protective and territorial; Collies will herd anything they come across, and ever hopeful terriers will dig up your yard in search of vermin. It is not an accident that Irish Setters don't herd sheep and Doberman Pinschers are not used to hunt pheasant. In their classic study, *Genetics and the Social Behavior of the Dog* (1965), researchers John Paul Scott and John L. Fuller discovered that even when fed and treated exactly alike, Basenjis and Cocker Spaniels largely retained the specific behavior patterns characteristic of their respective breeds. Years later, Dr. Raymond Coppinger and Richard Schneider tried very hard to teach Border Collies to guard sheep rather than herd them and livestock guardian dogs to herd them instead of protect them. They had absolutely no success whatsoever, although the dogs were raised in a controlled environment just for this purpose.

What *does* make a good herding dog, then? Earlier, I mentioned that physical traits are generally ruled by just a handful of genes. The same cannot be said for behavior. Behaviors are usually influenced by a number of genes, as well as by early life experiences, current environmental factors, and even possible physical ailments. Dr. Elaine Ostrander, for example, a molecular geneticist with the Dog Genome Project, worked to isolate the specific genes responsible for herding behavior in Border Collies and the Newfoundland's passion for

From Wolf to Dog: Alertness and Fearfulness

Researchers believe that our human ancestors worked very hard to change two major wolf attributes into more dog-like qualities. These characteristics are alertness and fearfulness, traits that are critical to survival in the wild but that hinder domesticity. This is why the average dog greets strangers happily rather than running away from them or biting them. It is also why more than one dog has been able to sleep peacefully while a burglar ransacks the house. It's a thin line we are trying to walk—we want our dogs to tell us when something is "not right" but meet and greet our friends with quiet pleasure. We also expect our dogs to discern which is which—even when we aren't sure ourselves. After all, your possessions are more likely to be "borrowed" unlawfully by your brother-in-law than by a complete stranger.

Behaviors are usually influenced by a number of genes, as well as by early life experiences, current environmental factors, and even physical ailments.

swimming. Ostrander and her colleagues concluded that a *number* of genes is responsible for each behavior. Show dogs are evaluated on looks (hair type, size, length of muzzle, etc.), each factor of which is controlled by one, or at the most, a few genes. Hunting behavior, on the other hand, is complex and depends on a large number of genetic factors that have to work together to make the behavior "happen." No amount of training, diet, and opportunity can make up for a lack of the right genes, as Coppinger and company found out.

It all goes back to selective breeding and its remolding of natural wolf behavior. While many working dogs retain their wolf-like aggression, the original lupine predatory behavior pattern is purposely disrupted at certain points. For example, this is the normal sequence a wolf uses to get dinner:

- orient to target (actively seek out appropriate prey)
- get a fix ("eye") on the prey
- stalk the prey
- chase the prey
- grab/bite the prey

Independent thinking—characteristic of hunting breeds like Beagles—is a type of intelligence.

- kill the prey
- tear apart and eat the prey

Dog breeders have tinkered around with this ancient system and disrupted the pattern to get dogs to omit, revise, redirect, or enhance certain elements of it. Herding dogs, for instance, retain (or even enhance) the predatory "eye," stalk, and chase, but they are supposed to stop short of grabbing and biting their charges. Some types of cattle-dogs are bred to carry the kill pattern further—into the "grab/bite" stage. Pointing dogs are bred only to carry the kill pattern as far as eye and stalk (which is then followed by the "point" stance). However, the point itself is hardwired into this group of dogs. They can't be trained to hunt until they "show point," and they can't be *trained* to show point at all—they just do it.

Sheep guardian dogs turn their aggression to "outsiders," often including humans. They may tolerate their owners but are not usually very affectionate to them. This makes them different from herders and retrievers, who work extremely closely with people. Hounds work more independently and are thus less "loyal," while pointers are somewhere in the middle. They are more independent than retrievers but less so than hounds.

Scott and Fuller also tested the independent thinking ability of various breeds and concluded that hunting dogs like Beagles rated much higher on this scale than Shetland Sheepdogs. This may seem surprising because Shelties are generally considered "smarter" than Beagles; however, Shelties are bred to obey their owners. Dog obedience trainers rank Border Collies, Poodles, German Shepherd Dogs, Golden Retrievers, and Doberman Pinschers, in that order, as the smartest, but they were testing for a particular skill set mostly involving obedience rather than problem-solving ability, which demands a different sort of intelligence. (I am not saying that Golden Retrievers aren't good problem solvers; what I am saying is that obedience instructors typically don't rate a dog on that criterion.) Labrador Retrievers are commonly rated highly intelligent, but astute trainers correctly recognize that they while they are enthusiastic and eager to please, their actual IQ is barely average. There is a difference between "trainability" (at which Shelties and Poodles excel) and independent thinking—characteristic of hunting types like Beagles. Which measures true "intelligence"? I guess it depends on what you want in a breed.

Breeders have succeeded beyond anyone's wildest dreams, producing an eye-popping, jaw-dropping parade of canine varieties: We have Great Danes and Great Pyrenees, Black and Tan Coonhounds and Black Russian Terriers, Australian Cattle Dogs and Australian Terriers, Bulldogs and Bullmastiffs, Chinese Cresteds and Chinese Shar-Peis, and innumerable pointers, setters, retrievers, spaniels, and hounds. What we do with them now that most of us don't really need them to guard, hunt, herd, or pull—all the things we bred them for—is proving interesting. And challenging.

Chapter 4

Training Basics

As dog owners and dog lovers, it's up to us to maximize our pets' chance for a healthy and happy life. This can only be accomplished by communicating to them what kind of conduct we require. That's training in a nutshell. Your dog doesn't have to know how to fetch slippers, play dead, or bake a meringue pie to be well trained. If he listens to you reliably and understands commands like *sit* and *come*, you're well on your way to a more fulfilling relationship with your best friend. Most dogs want to do the right thing. We just need to help them understand what that is.

Reward-Based Training

I saw a cartoon once in which two dogs were meeting for the first time. One of them said excitedly, "Hi there! My name is No-No Bad Dog, what's yours?" This captures the essence of what most dogs hear from their owners every day, all day. "No!" "Stop it, you crazy mutt!" "No!" "No!" "No!" Unfortunately for dogs, most people have the idea that a good dog is one who does nothing at all. That's because the things dogs like to do, such as barking, chasing, digging, and chewing, are frowned upon by their clueless owners.

Wise owners know that trying to extinguish such behaviors is either useless or results in depressed, anxious pets. Instead, they know how to channel their dog's natural energy into positive behaviors. That's the key: positive.

Technically speaking, "positive training" includes anything an owner actually does to change a dog's behavior, so whacking him over the head with a two-by-four to get him to stop chasing the cat is classified as "positive punishment." But in common parlance, and in this book, we'll restrict the term "positive training" to "reward-based training."

Reward-based training means encouraging a dog to do what you want by giving him a little gift when he does it, such as praise or a small treat. A similar idea is "luring" or "bribing" your dog—which means tempting him with a treat or other reward *before* he does what you want. It's used, for example, to get a dog to go into a crate or perform some other activity he's not at all sure he wants to do. Reward-based training works because it makes a dog feel good rather than bad. When dogs feel good, they are more responsive, more obedient, and learn better.

A note on rewards: As your dog responds more and more quickly, make

> Reward-based training means encouraging a dog to do what you want by giving him a little gift when he does it, such as praise or a small treat.

the treat or other reward intermittent; you can replace it sometimes with "Good boy!" and sometimes with nothing. Keep him guessing. Believe it or not, the use of intermittent rewards has been shown to produce better results than using constant rewards. The uncertainty factor seems to be a powerful incentive. Maybe that's why so many people play the lottery.

Punishment

The opposite of a reward is a punishment. Punishment simply means using a negative consequence to correct a dog's misbehavior. It does have a place in dog training when it takes the form of so called "negative punishment," as long as it is mild and does not cause physical pain or mental anguish. Negative punishment means taking something pleasant away from a dog's environment to get him to change his ways. One example would be to stop petting him when he is pawing at you for attention. This is a negative consequence and so can be classified as punishment. It can be very effective.

Good leaders use reward-based training to motivate their dogs.

Positive punishment requires action on the part of an owner. It is generally more severe than negative punishment. One common example might be jerking a leash attached to a choke collar. It goes all the way up the scale to the aforementioned whacking with a two-by-four and worse.

While positive punishment seems to be our natural reaction to all sorts of misbehavior, it is usually ill-advised and for many reasons:

• Dogs associate pain with the person who is wielding it—not with their own behavior.
• Pain or loud noises flood the dog with all kinds of stress hormones that actually inhibit learning.
• Physical punishment makes aggressive dogs MORE aggressive.
• Fearful dogs who are physically punished become MORE fearful.
• Even if punishment seems to stop the objectionable behavior, it's only a temporary hiatus.
• The behavior may be redirected to another person.
• The behavior may continue when the punisher is not present.

In short, dogs who are angry, afraid, or confused cannot learn anything except to become angrier, more fearful, and more confused. The same is true for the trainer. Good leaders do not intimidate, yell, throw things, or snarl. They lead. Angry, fearful, or confused trainers can't teach anything to anyone. Hitting a dog makes about as much sense as hitting a child—and it's inhumane to boot.

Six Rules for Change

Creating a healthy relationship with a dog should be based not on punishment but on mutual respect and affection. Because you are the owner, the human, and the one legally responsible (and the smart one, right?), it's up to you to set the parameters so that this desirable state of affairs can actually take place.

1. Commit Yourself to the Relationship

Studies have shown over and over that the single most important component in creating a healthy owner–dog relationship is commitment on the part of the owner. Your dog does not give up on you. Don't give up on him. His bad behavior is not personally directed at you—it's a tactic he has developed as a mechanism to get what he thinks he needs. That's all it is. It generally takes about 30 days, even with good training, for a dog to develop a new (correct) habit.

2. Honor Your Breed

Terriers, hounds, and retrievers have different mindsets and will develop differently. Respect the difference. Soft, gentle, quiet people usually do best with a dog with a similar temperament. Tough, strong, more independent breeds thrive with stronger, more no-nonsense owners. This doesn't mean violent or abusive—it means firm and in control. A training technique that works well with a person-oriented breed like a retriever may not work with an independent breed like a hound or terrier.

Creating a healthy relationship with a dog should be based on mutual respect and affection.

3. Accentuate Good Behavior by Using Rewards

Timing is everything. Your best chance of correcting inappropriate behavior is to respond immediately to appropriate actions. Trainers call rewards "reinforcers" for a very good reason: They reinforce the desired behavior. Some trainers use clickers, which act as a bridge at first between the desired action and the reward; a quick click on the clicker is a notice to the dog that a reward is coming. However, it works just as well to quickly say "Good dog!" (using the same words every time) and follow with a more substantive reward.

4. Never Hurt Your Dog

As mentioned earlier, hurting a dog is a hindrance to learning. It is sickening to think of the number of dogs who have been choked, shocked, hit, screamed at, isolated, shoved, and had their noses rubbed in you-know-what on the principle of "training." Dogs who are fearful or in pain cannot internalize good behavior. They will only try to avoid the pain. The immediate inappropriate behavior may appear to stop, but it will only be redirected. Dogs associate punishment with the person who does it, not with the targeted behavior.

When attempting to solve a problem behavior, create a calm environment enriched by exercise, affection, and training.

5. Give Your Dog the Chance to Learn

Create a calm environment enriched by exercise, affection, and training. Bored, lonely, isolated, frightened, and stressed dogs are unhappy dogs headed for trouble.

6. Establish Expectations

Your dog can learn only if he knows what is really expected of him. This can be accomplished only when 1. the dog pays attention to you; and 2. the dog trusts you. If either component is missing, the relationship is headed for trouble. Establishing expectations means doing so for yourself, as well as for your dog. Remember, your dog is a dog—not a human being, cat, wolf, robot, or toy. Do not expect him to be something other than what he is.

A trained dog is responsive, polite, and safe to be around.

Basic Training

A trained dog is a wonderful addition to the family. He is responsive, polite, and safe to be around. And while dogs are not necessarily naturals at this, it's not difficult to hone their social skills by teaching them simple training basics.

Look at Me! or Watch Me!

The very first command every dog should learn is *look at me* or *watch me*. This command redirects his behavior from whatever is distracting him to where it belongs: you. By the way, dogs can read faces, something no other non-human animal has been shown to do. So keep smiling. When a dog is focused on you and thereby paying attention, your commands are much more likely to yield positive results.

How to Teach Look at Me! or Watch Me!

1. Keep some treats at hand. Say "Watch me!" or "Look at me!"
2. He'll probably look up just because you've made a noise. Give him the treat.

Note: This "trick" usually takes about five seconds for a dog to learn. However, some dogs (such as hounds, who are generally more interested in smelling the ground) may be disinclined to look up. Keep trying. Also, start this training in a quiet atmosphere with no distractions. You can then bring him into a more social or exciting environment.

What Not to Do: Don't fall into the trap of bribing your dog by showing him the treat first. You want him to make contact with you, not the reward.

Sit

When a dog is sitting, he is not jumping up, running away, or digging. That alone makes this a worthwhile command. It is just easier for a dog to stay still while he is sitting down. It can also help a dog to learn his place in the family (which is not the boss position).

How to Teach *Sit*

Sit is one of the easiest commands to teach.

1. Simply take a treat and hold it above your dog's nose.
2. Say "Sit" and slowly pass the treat back over his head.
3. He will automatically sit down, naturally lift up his head, and plunk his rear on the floor.
4. Praise him quickly and hand him the treat.

   Note: As with other commands, gradually replace the food reward with praise.

   What Not to Do: People used to teach dogs to sit by pushing down on their rear ends while saying "Sit." Most contemporary trainers agree that this level of force is not needed and could even damage a dog's hips.

Come

In formal terms, the *come* command is also known as the *recall*. It's the most important command of all because your dog's life may depend on it. It is also in many ways the most difficult. That's because people often don't bother thinking about its importance until their dog is galloping

The *sit* is one of the easiest commands for a dog to learn.

down the street in the opposite direction after a car or a squirrel. By then it is too late.

How to Teach Come

It is best to teach this command with your dog on the end of a long leash. You don't want to give him the option of making a mistake. You also want to pick a calm, quiet time when he has had some exercise. Don't start it when he is running around the house like a crazy person.

1. Kneel down, with your arms open. Start by calling your dog's name and the word "Come!" in a happy, bright voice.
2. If he comes to you, praise him and give him a treat or favorite toy.

It's best to teach the *come* command with your dog on the end of a long leash.

3. If he takes a few steps and stops, lure him with the offer of food.

   Note: If you have an older dog who has trained himself to ignore the word "come" as a command, try a different word like "here!" or anything at all that is novel. Keep the session short and happy, and follow with playtime so that he associates having a good time with being at your side.

   What Not to Do: Never, ever call a dog to you to punish him or do anything he might not like, such as a bath. Doing so may make him less likely to want to come to you in the future.

Down

The purpose of the *down* command is to keep a dog in a comfortable, relaxed position. It is an important base command for other work (and trick training), and it also helps establish your leadership. (Being "down" is a submissive position in the dog world.) It also acts as a safety valve—a lying dog will find it more difficult to get up and race into oncoming traffic.

How to Teach Down

1. Begin with your dog in a sitting position. It may be a good idea to get down on the same level as your dog if he seems unsure or reluctant to perform the required action.

2. Hold a treat right in front of his nose and gradually lower it toward the floor while saying "Down" or "Drop." This is sometimes called the "magnet" method.

Note: As with other commands, gradually make the rewards intermittent.

What Not to Do: Some trainers suggest pulling the dog's legs forward to get the dog into place, but I have not found that very effective. Nor it is a good idea to pull on the collar, which could harm him. Also, do not try to force the dog down by pressing on his shoulders—that's a move that sets up an automatic resistance.

Stay

Technically, all dogs should sit or stay down until released, but the *stay* command helps the dog understand that the release word may not occur for a while. (In the *down* command, particularly, many dogs tend to bounce up as soon as they have succeeded.) This command should be taught after *sit*, *down*, and the release word.

How to Teach Stay

1. While your dog is sitting, say "Stay" in a firm clear voice and hold your hand palm outward.
2. Take one step backward and wait briefly—usually just a couple of seconds at first.
3. Say the release word.
4. Give him a treat.
5. Progress by taking further backward steps, introducing distractions, and adding in a longer wait time.

Note: If he doesn't succeed, just do not give the treat. Eventually, you should be able to take 20 steps back or even get out of his sight for several minutes. Some obedience dogs are asked to stay for half an hour.

What Not to Do: Don't become impatient. This command takes a long

Walking should be a pleasant, fun experience for both you and your dog.

The *leave it* command can prevent your dog from getting his paws on something poisonous (like the grapes pictured here) or otherwise potentially dangerous.

time to master. If you want your dog to be patient, you need to be patient as well.

Walk Nicely on Leash

The basic idea behind leash training is that you can walk your dog, not vice versa. Walking should be a pleasant, fun experience for both of you.

How to Teach *Walk Nicely on Leash*

Begin when he is well exercised and a little tired. As always, pick a quiet place free from distractions.

1. Use a simple buckle collar, not a choke chain.
2. Hold a treat at his nose level.
3. Praise and treat him when he walks with you.
4. If he stops or tries to forge ahead, just stop quietly and say his name, offering a treat if you must. He should come right back to you.

    Note: Problems in leash walking are dealt with in Chapter 22.

    What Not to Do: Don't drag, choke, or yell at your dog. Making a walk an unpleasant experience will only multiply your difficulties.

Leave It

More often than you ever want to know, your dog will take something that you don't want him to have—baby's diapers, carving knives, snakes, a dead rat, or your best pair of flip flops. Getting him to leave such things alone will be an object of first importance.

How to Teach *Leave It*

Begin in a distraction-free environment.

1. Hide a piece of dog biscuit in one hand, and keep something really yummy like a piece of sausage or other high-value treat in the other.

2. Open your hand to reveal the biscuit. When your dog tries to eat it, say "Leave it" and shut your hand. About one second later, offer him the better treat.
3. Practice over and over. Later, you can offer both treats in different places, like on the floor. (If he tries to get it, put your foot over it.) The idea is to get him to understand that a reward is in the offing.

This is one behavior for which you should offer the trade as often as possible. You want your dog to be confident that when he leaves something as asked there is something in it for him.

Note: Similar to *leave it* is *drop it*. In the latter case, the offensive item is actually in the dog's mouth, but the training steps are the same. Let him chew on something of minor interest, say "Drop it!" and offer the high-value treat. Start with less desirable things and move to more desirable things. I have to say that some items (like stolen steak from the counter) are so desirable that you'll have to count yourself lucky if your dog listens to you.

What Not to Do: Don't tease your dog. Always offer him a valuable trade for what you are denying him.

Release Word

Your dog will need to know when it is okay to stop sitting, lying down, or whatever you have asked him to do. This is why you'll need to pick a "release word" to free him from his duty. The release command can be taught at the same time that the other obedience commands are taught.

A release word will help your dog know when he's free to get up from whatever position you've asked him to hold.

In serious problem behavior cases, you may have to consult with a professional trainer or behaviorist.

How to Teach a Release Word

Choose a simple one-syllable word that you don't normally use otherwise. Choices might include "Free!", "Break!", "Joy!" or anything you want. It's tempting to use body language to bolster the word command, and it's a good starting point, but the goal is eventually to get your dog to respond solely to a verbal command (unless, of course, he is deaf). Otherwise he'll be taking off if you just turn your head—not a good idea.

1. Have your dog on a leash.
2. Say that your dog is sitting. When you are ready to allow him to get up, say the release word in a bright cheerful voice: "Free!"
3. Praise and reward him.

   Practice several times a day for about five minutes each time.

   Note: If he doesn't spring up immediately, use the leash to gently guide him to your side and then walk off happily with him.

   What Not to Do: The word "okay" as a release word is not a good choice. You probably say it too much. And try to find something that other dog owners don't use either. If you're in an obedience class or other group activity, you'll want to have your own word so that your dog doesn't get distracted by anyone else's commands.

Professional Help

Many people benefit from going to professional training classes to help hone their dog training skills. Dogs learn basic obedience and socialization skills, and their owners learn how to handle their dogs before problems get out of hand. (Don't expect to ship your dog off somewhere, though, and have a perfect animal returned to you. You have to learn together.) Your veterinarian or local kennel club can help you locate a good trainer in your area. The Association of Pet Dog Trainers (www.apdt.com) is another excellent resource.

Although this book is designed to help you deal with typical dog problems yourself, some owners and their dogs need professional assistance. Help comes in different forms—the trick is to find the right person for your particular problem. Serious aggression, in particular, must be handled by a qualified professional; many ordinary dog trainers are not equipped to deal with it. If you are very lucky, you may be able to locate a veterinary behaviorist who can not only give training advice but prescribe behavioral medications when needed. Unfortunately, there are very few of them. A regular vet, however, can work with a trainer to accomplish much the same thing. Another option is to locate a certified animal behaviorist. A list of such qualified people can be found at the Animal Behaviorist Society's website (www.animalbehaviorsociety.org).

Luckily, most people can learn techniques to deal with problems themselves. This book is a handy tool to help you do just that.

Chapter 5

Aggression: Human

Aggression can be defined as violence or the threat of violence and is the most common and the most troubling problem behavior in dogs. Aggression, in ascending order of seriousness, includes growling, snarling, snapping, and out-and-out biting.

While some rough play among puppies is normal, extremely rough play behavior may signal a dog without proper socialization skills.

Aggression toward human beings is the number-one reason why dogs are euthanized in this country. In fact, the United States reports the highest incidence of dog aggressiveness in the world, with an estimated 4.5 million dog attack victims each year. All dogs have teeth, and all dogs, even the nicest, can bite under the right (or wrong) circumstances. If you haven't been bitten by a dog yourself, you surely know someone who has.

The typical aggressive dog is purebred, young, male, and intact (unneutered). In fact, between 70 and 90 percent of reported canine aggression incidents are committed by intact males. They bite twice as often as females and cause more serious injuries. The difference in aggression levels between males and females appears very soon after birth. Among the fair sex, unaltered females are more likely to be aggressive than their spayed counterparts.

Aggression usually emerges when dogs are between six months and four years of age, with the most serious injuries caused by dogs between one and four years. The earlier a dog shows signs of aggression, the more serious the problem. While some rough play among puppies is normal, extremely rough play behavior may signal a "tone-deaf" dog without proper socialization skills. This behavior may be genetically driven.

Types of Aggression

Aggression takes many overlapping forms, including dominance aggression, fear/pain aggression, and resource guarding. In many cases, there is more than one motivation—a dog could be angry *and* fearful *and* protective *and* in pain all at once. In some cases, aggression is limited to attacks on other animals, including fellow dogs (see Chapter 6: Aggression: Dog–Dog), while in other cases, a dog will display aggression to people as well. When aggressive behaviors are not dealt with correctly and in a timely manner, they tend to get worse— more frequent, more intense, and spread to a wider range of circumstances.

Dominance Aggression

Dominance aggression is commonly referred to as aggressive behavior designed to maintain an "alpha" position in the pack. It is not clear how dominance is related to aggression, but I can tell you that even when it plays a part, it is, like all other factors, directly related to underlying stress. It may be that dominant behavior, which seems so tightly linked to aggression, is in itself a way to handle stress—a kind of "middle manager" syndrome.

The whole idea of dominance was initiated in 1922, by a Norwegian researcher named Thorleif Schjelderup-Ebbe. He worked with hierarchy in, of all things, chickens. His work revealed that chickens compete with each other for status as much as they do for food and mates. Most modern researchers believe that his work still has some value for canids, especially wild

Fear aggression is aggressive behavior that stems from fear or anxiety.

ones like wolves, where males and females each establish their own dominance lines.

However, the concept of dominance aggression is a controversial one. Some behavior experts claim that this behavior does not even exist, while others assert that it is a normal part of dog behavior. It is a hotly contended topic.

Fear Aggression

Fear aggression is exactly what it sounds like: aggressive behavior that stems from fear or anxiety. This is, in many ways, the most "excusable" type of aggression, as we too are apt to feel snappish and out of sorts when we are ill or frightened. It is a natural response to extreme circumstances.

Resource Guarding

Resource guarding occurs when a dog attempts to defend what he regards as "his" with aggressive behavior. Resource guarding may begin with a food bowl and widen to include sleeping areas, toys, and even human beings. Many people think that a dog who guards his owner is being protective. This is true in one sense, of course. But it often means that the dog regards the human as a valuable possession, like the couch, toy, or food bowl, to be kept from others and remain the dog's personal "property." In other words, owner-guarding behavior may not be aimed at protecting you but instead at keeping you, his favorite possession, away from other people. This is why many dogs who "guard" people are just as likely to bite the person's child or spouse as a complete stranger. (On the upside, this is another example of natural behavior that can be redirected in the case of guard dogs to ward off evildoers.)

Nearly all forms of dog aggression are caused by stress.

Causes

Nearly all forms of aggression are caused by stress, a condition familiar to us 21st-century humans. Stress is a response to any event that disturbs the equilibrium. Stress can manifest itself as a physical, mental, or emotional reaction. It can make us fearful, angry, confused, or sad. It can make people violent. It can make dogs bite.

What causes stress? In the wild, stress results from competition for food or mates; in civilization, it includes crowding, inconsistent training, a chaotic environment, and overly emotional or abusive owners. It is the product of uncertainty and fear. Mother dogs become aggressive when they fear for their pups' safety, feeding dogs protect their bowls for fear of losing out on dinner, and territorial dogs fight to protect a favored place they fear losing. Even maintaining a threatened position in a hierarchy can be accompanied by intense feelings of stress, as anyone who has worked for a living knows.

Stress inhibits the cerebral cortex, the part of the brain that enables dogs to learn, but it activates the primitive limbic system, which allows them to react quickly without thinking. So when a dog is stressed, he is much more likely to react than to think things through. A highly reactive dog can be a very aggressive one.

Aggression is a perfectly normal and protective response to stress. It is natural in both wolves and dogs. However, from the human standpoint, such behaviors are not tolerated. We don't want a "natural" dog—we want a civilized one. Breeders have spent many centuries trying to tamp down aggression in dogs altogether or redirect it to "acceptable" targets, like strangers for guard dogs or specific prey for hunting dogs.

Nearly all the causes of aggression I list below are stressors in one way or another. Luckily, it really doesn't matter too much why your dog is acting badly. It's hard to read a dog's mind, and it turns out that aggressive dogs generally respond

Dogs suffering from pain are more likely to bite than are healthy dogs.

well to treatment that reduces stress: good medical care, stable leadership, and targeted reshaping techniques.

Medical Conditions

A great number of medical conditions can lead to a dog becoming aggressive. When a previously gentle dog starts behaving aggressively, a thorough physical is in order. Here are some of the most common medical causes of aggression in dogs.

- **Pain.** It is well known that dogs suffering from pain are more likely to bite than are healthy dogs. Pain is a number-one stressor. Arthritis, neck and back injuries, digestive ills, wounds, prostatic inflammation, or even a general malaise can contribute to the tendency to bite.

- **Sex hormonal imbalances.** Hormone imbalances, especially high levels of testosterone, can lead to aggression.

- **Phobias and fears.** Frightened dogs are stressed and unstable and are more likely to bite.

- **Vision problems.** Dogs who can't see well are uncertain and stressed. They are likely to lash out at unfamiliar people or animals.

- **Neurological problems.** These can include brain tumors (most common in geriatric dogs), viral or bacterial encephalitis, epilepsy (dogs are most likely to be aggressive in the post-seizure phase, and aggression may occur in dogs with partial seizures whose signs are so slight the owner does not notice them), and head traumas.

- **Thyroid malfunction.** Some aggressive dogs have borderline low thyroid hormone levels. These canines often display aggression that does not conform to any normal patterns. Although the thyroid function may technically be in the normal range, once it is boosted to optimum levels by inexpensive thyroid hormone replacement therapy, aggression levels drop considerably. Certain breeds of dogs, like Shetland Sheepdogs and Golden Retrievers, are especially prone to this problem.

- **Hypoglycemia.** Hypoglycemia, or low blood sugar, can cause aggression or anxious behavior.

- **Malnutrition.** Dogs suffering from extreme hunger or malnutrition may become anxious about potential interference in their food. This can also occur in dogs who have had a history of starvation, even if they are being well fed now. It is a problem that frequently occurs in rescued dogs.

- **Depression.** Recent research from Zaragoza University in Spain suggests that some aggressive dogs may even be clinically depressed. Aggressive dogs often have lower than normal levels of the "feel-good" brain chemicals serotonin and dopamine, neurotransmitters that help offset "stress hormones" like cortisol.

Recent research suggests that some aggressive dogs may even be clinically depressed.

Wolf Heritage

Aggression is part of dogs' natural inheritance. As in their ancestor wolves, it serves (along with running away) as a means to resolve conflict. Different circumstances require different responses. In other words, wolves are aggressive when they need to be so. When they don't, they aren't—it's a huge waste of energy. And wolves cannot afford to waste energy. (When they do occur, fights among wolves are usually *very* brief and are engaged in as a last resort.) Dogs, on the other hand, especially well-fed, well-housed domestic dogs, seem to have a lot of energy to waste and often get into trouble that a wolf would avoid. At any rate, the following stressors cause aggression in both dogs and wolves:

- **Resources.** A dog's tendency to guard what's important comes directly from his lupine heritage. Food, for example, is a precious resource and wolves protect their kill vigorously, especially when it is scarce. Wolves also guard their mates and favorite places. Your dog may do the same.
- **Territory.** Aggression over territory is especially pronounced in the wolf world, especially when there is a lot of competition for food. Wolves display aggression toward intruders within their home territory, and some of their descendants do the same. Wolves and dogs are wanderers by nature, and so the "territory" may include not just your house but other places where your dog

is regularly walked. In other cases, the "territory" might be restricted to his bed. Dogs with territorial aggression may first display it when they are between 16 and 20 weeks of age, the same period at which phobias develop. This is the age at which young wolves begin moving away from their dens and experience new things, so they are in a period of generally heightened awareness. With a rescued dog, his new owner may see no signs of territorial aggression until he has been in his new home about three weeks, at which point he decides that this territory belongs to him.

- **Status.** Social animals like wolves protect their place in the pack and so do dogs, although not all dogs have inherited a strong pack identity. In a wolf pack, there are two separate lines of dominant animals: one for males and one for females. When dogs do form a "pack," it's usually all mixed up, partially because a group of dogs is usually unrelated.
- **Self-defense.** Wolves will, of course, fight to protect themselves and their offspring. And so will dogs.
- **Bullying.** Despite our romantic notions about the nobility of wolves, they have a sad tendency to push around low-ranking pack members. So do some dogs. And with dogs, the low-ranking member may include humans as well as other canines.
- **Social status.** Wolves test each other's character and exploit each other's weaknesses and uncertainties, which leads to advancement within the pack. Guess what? Your dog can do the same thing. And he may do it with you.

Breed Predilection and Genetics

We already know that aggression is related to lower levels of serotonin and dopamine. And interestingly, a recent doctoral study has revealed a variation in the genes related to serotonin and dopamine in dogs. In other words, aggressive behavior can be inherited. If either parent of a litter of puppies has aggressive tendencies, the likelihood is high that some or all of the puppies will inherit this behavior. Furthermore, this type of inherited aggression shows up within the first six

Breeds that may have a higher than average number of individuals with fear aggression include Border Collies and Australian Shepherds.

or seven weeks of life. This seems true for both dominance- and fear-related aggression.

However, the degree to which aggression is controlled by genetic heritage is fiercely debated, usually with more heat than light. It is my conviction that some breeds tend to be aggressive, although this statement is sometimes regarded as politically incorrect. But how could this not be true? Breeding matters, and dogs of breeds that were developed to be aggressive often turn out to be that way.

- **Purposeful breeding.** For some breeds, breeders instilled territorial aggression (guard dogs); in other cases, dogs were bred to fight other dogs; and so on. Territorial breeds include Akitas and Airedales. Fighting dogs include "pit bulls," Chow Chows, and Chinese Shar-Peis. Rottweilers and Alaskan Malamutes, too, were historically bred to be aggressive. Fighting lines of pit bull terriers have been deliberately selected for their eagerness to engage in combat, whether against fellow dogs, other animals, or even humans. Breeds that may have a higher than average number of individuals with fear aggression include German Shepherd Dogs, Border Collies, and Australian Shepherds—all are highly reactive, sensitive breeds.

- **Poor breeding practices.** While guard dogs and fighting dogs were specifically bred for aggression,

SMART STUFF

Is There a "Bite Gene"?

There is no "bite gene," no specific genetic marker that accounts for aggressive behavior. There is, however, a genetic base for reactivity, which in some cases can lead to aggression, and in others, to phobias.

Breeds most likely to snap at children include West Highland White Terriers and Yorkshire Terriers.

other breeds have been unfortunate victims of poor breeding practices. In these cases, the breed is not supposed to be aggressive, but inattention to correct temperament has allowed poor behavioral traits to slip through. For a long time (ever since the classic movie *Lady and the Tramp*), Cocker Spaniels had a bad reputation in this regard; fortunately, responsible breeders are working hard to retrieve the breed's naturally sweet disposition. Recently, Dalmatians were also afflicted with the instant popularity curse of a hit movie and have yet to recover emotionally.

Which is the breed *most* prone to aggression? Pit bulls? Nope. Rottweilers? Uh-uh. German Shepherds? Negative. Chow Chows? Sorry. A new study conducted by the University of Pennsylvania and published in *Applied Animal Behavior Science* analyzing 33 breeds has pegged the Dachshund the most aggressive breed. The study showed that 1 in 5 Dachshunds has bitten or tried to bite strangers, a like number has attacked other dogs, and 1 in 12 has snapped at his owner. Other small breeds follow the Dachshund in aggressive behavior: Number two on the list is the tiny Chihuahua, and number three is the Parson Russell/Jack Russell Terrier. Breeds most likely to snap at kids include Scottish Terriers, Miniature Schnauzers, West Highland White Terriers, Yorkshire Terriers, Fox Terriers, Lhasa Apsos, and Pomeranians. These toy breeds in general tend to be somewhat snappish, if only because they are so small that the looming world around them may appear a very dangerous place. After all, there's no defense like a good offense. In addition, owners and breeders sometimes take a far too lackadaisical attitude toward them—after all, they are so tiny—how much harm can they do?

Why is it that nobody knows about the danger of smaller dogs—or if they do know, they don't care? The reason, obviously, is that these dogs often inflict such insignificant bites that emergency medical attention is not sought, and the incident doesn't make the record books. An aggressive German Shepherd Dog, American Pit Bull Terrier, Chow Chow, or Siberian Husky is much more likely to inflict serious damage than a Dachshund and therefore gets more press. Breeds scoring low for aggression include Basset Hounds, Golden Retrievers, Labrador Retrievers, and Greyhounds. Setters and other breeds developed to retrieve upland game fowl were specifically bred to have lower levels of aggression.

When we consider fatal (and officially recorded) dog attacks, the evidence is clear. In a late 20th-century report involving 101 such attacks, fully 43 percent of the attacks were perpetuated by pit bulls or pit bull mixes. German Shepherd Dogs and their mixes accounted for 15 percent of the attacks; Siberian Huskies, Malamutes, and mixes accounted for 18 percent; and Doberman Pinschers, Rottweilers, and wolf hybrids each were responsible for 5 percent. These figures are significantly greater than the representation of such breeds in the general dog population.

The important thing to remember is that any dog of any breed can be aggressive, and breed and type are not always accurate predictors of behavior. Indeed, many formerly fearsome breeds, including the Mastiff and Doberman Pinscher, have had their temperaments deliberately "softened" by careful breeders who understand that these dogs largely function as pets, not guard dogs, in today's world.

THE EXPERT SAYS

Peggy Swager, well-known trainer, behaviorist consultant, and author of *Training the Hard to Train Dog* says, "Sometimes the aggression issue grows over time without the owner noticing. Typically, what has happened is the dog may start doing small things to pick up what I call 'leadership points.' The dog takes charge of areas in which the human being is supposed to control; after a time, the dog feels empowered enough (because he has enough leadership points) to take charge."

Environmental Factors

Your dog's environment plays the biggest role in shaping his behavior with regard to aggression. The wrong environment can make a naturally gentle dog mean, while the right one can keep a dog with aggressive tendencies on the straight and narrow. Here are some of the major environmental factors that produce aggression in dogs:

- **Stressful situations.** While a generally fearful dog's behavior may ultimately be grounded in

Dogs tend to become aggressive when they feel trapped and unable to escape from the approach of a stranger or threatening situation.

genetics, any dog can become fearful in a stressful situation. After all, dogs have limited ways to respond to a frightening situation. One of them is to bite what they deem to be the source. Although we often associate fear aggression with tiny dogs like Chihuahuas, the fearful, aggressive canine can be of any size. Dogs tend to become aggressive when they feel trapped and unable to escape from the approach of a stranger or threatening situation. Also, aggressive behavior can erupt when a dog is punished (or fears punishment) for house soiling or chewing.

Dogs are least stressed when they have clear expectations. The main expectation for your dog to learn is that all good things—food, exercise, and affection—come from you and that you are the decider as to when they happen. Dogs who can look confidently to their humans to supply their needs are least likely to turn aggressive.

- **Lack of structure and authority in the home.** This leads to uncertainty and more fearful behavior. Dogs appreciate the presence of a strong leader and a solid schedule. If there is a power vacuum, a potentially dominant dog may decide to take over a household.

- **Early imprinting by an aggressive/nervous mother dog.** It has been discovered (although it's not in the least surprising) that the social interaction between mother and pup during the weaning process has a strong effect on subsequent behavior. Simply put, a fearful mama dog will model fearful behavior to her pups, even if they haven't physically inherited specific genes for shyness or a tendency to aggression.

- **Past trauma or abuse.** This is especially the case for many rescued dogs. Bad experiences lead dogs to expect more bad experiences in the future. These pessimists are good candidates for biting.

- **Improper socialization.** Improper training of young dogs is an important factor in the development of aggression. When dogs are not socialized as puppies, especially during the critical socialization period (between 5 and 12 weeks of age), they can become aggressive in new situations. Puppies need to become accustomed to human touch, especially around the feet and head, at a very early age. They also need to make human friends. Puppies should meet at least 100 different people by the time they are 12 weeks old, including men and women of all ages, children, and people in wheelchairs, on bikes, and in uniform. For example, dogs who are not socialized to children at an early age can become fearful of them and become aggressive later.

- **Absence of bite inhibition.** Bite inhibition is a skill that puppies learn from their littermates. Because dogs lack hands, they explore the world with their mouths. When they nip too hard during play, the other puppies cry and stop playing. However, a puppy taken too soon from the litter may not have developed this critical social skill unless you teach it. Prepare to be nipped.

- **Overcrowding.** Crowding creates tension. Tension is accompanied by increased production of the hormone cortisol in the blood, and increased levels of cortisol are a contributing factor to aggression. Add to the mix the fact that dogs naturally compete for attention and it should come as no surprise that the more dogs a person has, the more likely it is that at least one of them will become aggressive.

An absence of bite inhibition in puppies can lead to more serious biting later in life.

- **Chaining or tethering.** Dogs who are chained or tethered are more likely to bite, although there is a chicken and egg thing going on here that is hard to decipher; it's not clear whether the chaining makes dogs more aggressive by removing the "flight" option from the fight-or-flight impulse or whether people are just in the habit of chaining up dangerous dogs.

- **Harsh training tools and techniques.** Use of harsh training tools, such as choke and pinch collars, can create pain when improperly applied—thus producing aggressive tendencies. So can yelling at a dog and frightening him.

- **Owner miscues.** Let's say that a dog growls at a stranger. If the owner says soothingly "It's okay, Fido," she has just (by her tone) rewarded the dog for growling. That wasn't the intent—but that's what the dog infers.

Because most bites occur to unattended children, it's important to supervise dog–child interactions.

What to Do

Dealing with an aggressive dog is difficult and in many cases may be beyond the skills of the ordinary pet owner. It also requires deep commitment to follow up and be consistent. In many cases, however, aggressive dogs can be "turned around."

1. **Take your dog to the vet.** Dogs who display aggression should first be taken to a vet for a complete medical checkup before any behavioral modification programs are initiated. Your dog may have a physical reason for his aggression; in that case, pain relievers or other medical treatment may completely eliminate the problem.

2. **See a qualified professional trainer/behaviorist.** If your dog does not have basic, humanely based obedience training, you need to start there. This will help you as much as it will help your dog. All dogs should respond to the basic commands: *look at me, come, sit, down, stay,* and *walk nicely on leash.* (See Chapter 4: Training Basics.) Credentialed animal behaviorists and veterinary behaviorists are ideal, but they are rare in some areas. That being said, many fine vets and trainers specialize in working with aggressive dogs, although they may lack formal qualifications. Find someone who eschews violence and who is experienced in working with aggressive dogs. Most dog obedience trainers do not want to handle them, and some regular obedience training designed for nonaggressive

dogs can actually make aggression worse. Unfortunately, you will not be able to simply send the dog off to a trainer and have him come back a different animal; you must be partners with your professional and continue the training at home as well. On the other hand, at least some of early anti-aggression training should ideally take place away from your home. A more neutral location is less likely to produce dominant or territorial behavior.

3. **Stay safe.** Your safety and that of your family must be your first consideration. It is most important to keep young children away from an aggressive dog. They are the ones who are most frequently and most severely bitten. If you are not able to keep yourself and loved ones secure by immediate management techniques, you may have to consider rehoming your dog.

4. **Supervise children.** Most bites occur to unattended children. The most common victim of a dog bite is a male child between nine and ten years of age, the same demographic likely to have the most intense interactions with dogs. These cases are very troubling, as there is often no way of knowing what triggered the bite, and invalid assumptions are made. Unless an adult was there to observe what happened, opposing statements like "The child did nothing at all to trigger an aggressive response" and "The child must have hurt the dog" are equally unsupported.

Have patience when dealing with an aggressive dog, and reward all gentle, nonaggressive behavior.

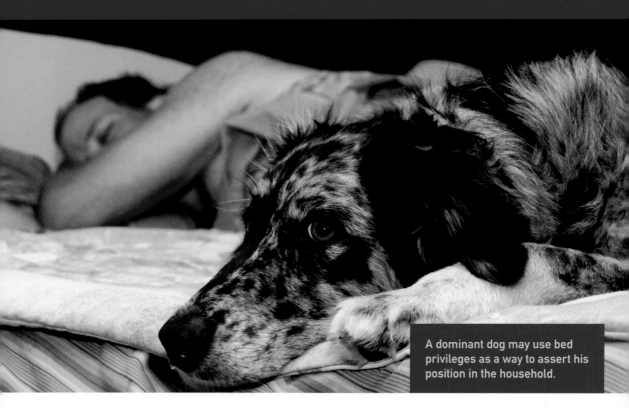

A dominant dog may use bed privileges as a way to assert his position in the household.

5. **Supervise your dog.** Most bites to strangers occur when your dog is left unattended. With you absent, the dog may feel free (or obligated) to protect his home any way he sees fit.

6. **Take notes.** Assess the level of aggression. Keep a log for at least a week, noting times, places, and specific circumstances or triggers associated with the behavior. If you can video-record the behavior, so much the better.

7. **Have male dogs neutered.** Aggressive tendencies in male dogs are triggered by the secretion of testosterone. About 30 percent of the time, castration eliminates or reduces aggression by at least 50 percent toward human family members. It does not matter at what age the castration is performed, so never think that it is "too late." Neutering male dogs is particularly effective in the most notorious of "biting breeds": German Shepherd Dogs, pit bulls, Chow Chows, and Rottweilers. (Castration is not as effective in human-aggressive dogs as it is in cases of aggression toward other animals.) On the other hand, female dogs who demonstrate aggressive tendencies fare better if they are not spayed before one year of age.

8. **Have patience.** This difficult behavior will not disappear quickly and may take months of work to bring under control. Set up small, incremental goals. Reward all gentle, nonaggressive behavior. If, for whatever reason, you can't afford to invest the necessary training time, you may have to rehome your dog.

9. **Get your family to cooperate.** Everyone in the household must be on board with the training; otherwise it is doomed to failure. The person who is the most consistent target of the dog's aggression must take an active role in the rehabilitation, unless, of course, that person is a very young child.

10. **Earn your dog's trust.** Aggressive dogs are stressed and fearful. Your goal is to make your home a safe-feeling place. Do this by modeling strong leadership skills and providing your dog with a safe, structured environment. Predictable, consistent behavior on your part will reduce stress in your dog. When he knows what to expect from you, he will be calmer, more confident, and less aggressive.

11. **Avoid the trigger.** Avoid as much as possible any situation that you know provokes aggression in your dog until your training program can address that specific situation. Many dogs express aggression only under specific circumstances: while on a leash, around children, near their food, and so on. Because safety is paramount, your first goal should be management—that is, limit or control the circumstances under which your dog tends to be aggressive. If your dog is food

Sometimes increasing a dog's exercise can help head off aggression.

SMART STUFF

Dog Body Language

While dogs don't use words, they can express themselves adequately with their body and vocalizations. Since even the smartest dog is unable to grasp some of the nuances of human speech, it's up to us to learn their language as best we can. It will always be an imperfect translation, but pidgin-dog-talk is better than nothing. Like other languages, dog talk has two components: vocabulary and syntax. With dogs, the vocabulary is his body parts: head, tail, back, and so forth—his syntax is the way he puts them together to make a sentence. For example, a wagging tail usually translates as happiness, but its speed and position can change the meaning entirely. Just as with human language, you must consider the context. Most of a dog's body language relates to how stressed or threatened he feels, and as I mention repeatedly, most canine aggression is related to stress and fear. Therefore, a careful reading of canine language can raise your own dog I.Q. and prevent an incident. Here is a quick lexicon:

Back: A stiff straight back can mean aggression. A hunched back indicates insecurity, fear, or submission.

Bowing: Most bowing is a play-eliciting behavior that can also be observed in courtship. However, a slightly different kind of bow, the "prey bow," can be observed just before an attack is initiated on a prey animal.

Drooling: Except in naturally drooling breeds like Basset Hounds and Saint Bernards, drooling often means sickness or fear.

Ears: Aggressive and frightened dogs lay their ears back—except in breeds like Beagles who have "dead," floppy ears that always remain droopy.

Eyebrows: Aggressive dogs frequently have prominent eyebrows; those of submissive dogs are usually barely discernible.

Eyes: Aggressive behavior is usually accompanied by a hard, intense stare; playing dogs will look away frequently. An averted gaze means submission or fear. Always look for the accompanying body posture for correct interpretation—a relaxed body postures suggests the dog is not aggressive, even if he is staring.

Forehead: Aggressive and stressed dogs often develop unsightly forehead lines (Botox, anyone?). Nonaggressive, mild-mannered types present a smooth, untroubled forehead to the world. With normally wrinkly faced dogs like Pugs, however, all bets are off.

Growling: According to the results of an animal-behavior study on growls (Farago, et al.), food guarding is the most clearly understood cue in canine society. Dogs can clearly distinguish between resource guarding growls (and take them more seriously) than threatening-a-stranger growls (males were instructed to stare menacingly at the dog to evoke the response) or playful growls (which tend to be much shorter and higher pitched than the other kinds). Human beings could not distinguish acoustical differences between the two serious kinds of growls, but dogs had no trouble at all. Recordings of the growls (placed behind a curtain near the target bone) were also used so that the dogs were not able to see the source of the growl and visually estimate their chances of taking the bone away. Apparently, dogs are much more serious about protecting their dinners than they are about threatening people. It makes sense that a threatened dog probably mixes his bravado with no small degree of fear, which a fellow canine can probably detect.

Hackles: A clear sign that something is amiss is raised hackles—the hairs on the dog's back. This is an involuntary reaction. Some dogs can raise their hackles from the neck to the root of the tail, which gives them an odd but trendy Mohawk look; other dogs can raise only their neck hackles or the neck and tail-base hackles. Longhaired dogs are handicapped in the hackle-raising department.

Mouth: Happy, relaxed dogs usually have open mouths with the corner slightly retracted, which is sort of a smile. And some dogs, especially herding breeds, actually grin, a rather frightening look that can be mistaken by humans for a snarl. However, grinning dogs have soft, half-closed eyes, rather than a hard stare. There will be no accompanying growl.

Grinning dogs may grin at visitors, which is doubly scary. They also grin at dinnertime. Dogs never grin at each other—only at human beings.

A yawn can signal opposite things. It can mean being tired, as with people, but it can also mean nervous energy. It is contagious among dogs too.

Dogs lick (or try to lick) human faces as a sign of affectionate subordination. In the wild, they do it to get food from higher-ups. When dogs lick their own noses, it is a gesture of appeasement or submission.

Neck: Aggressive dogs tend to have a stiff neck, while the necks of relaxed dogs tend to be more curved.

Stance: An aggressive dog usually stands tall, although the head and neck may be aligned with the back. In a play bow, the head is held noticeably lower than the tail.

Tail: Frightened dogs traditionally place their tails between their legs, but some dogs, like sight hounds, do that all the time. Beagles, on the other hand, traditionally carry their tails very high, which can be a sign of aggression in other breeds. A wagging tail does not always mean all is well, especially if the wagging tail is held low (usually means uncertainty) or "half-mast" (usually indicates aggression).

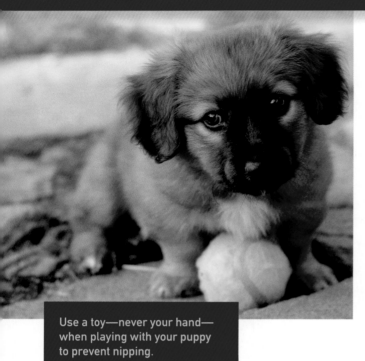

Use a toy—never your hand—when playing with your puppy to prevent nipping.

aggressive, for example, make sure that no one approaches his food bowl until you have resolved the problem. (In some cases, it works to remove the bowl entirely and feed the dog on the floor or even by hand.)

12. **Be careful with your approach.** If you must approach a dog who is stressed, do so quietly from the side in an arc, not head on. If he shows aggression, step back. Backing off is not the same as giving up or giving in. It is giving room. If your dog needs a lot of "personal space," it's a sign of his insecurity, not his dominance.

13. **Stand tall.** Dogs equate height with power, and they are much more likely to be nonconfrontational with people who use that natural height advantage. (This is another reason why children are more at risk than adults.)

14. **Take a "nothing is free" approach.** When training your aggressive dog, do not pet, stroke, or praise him unless he obeys a specific command, like *sit* or *down*. Totally ignore him otherwise. This is called the "nothing is free" approach. The best way to engineer this, however, is not to banish the dog to the outdoors. He won't make a connection that way. Keep him with you, but totally ignore him for a few hours. (Your dog may act quite oddly during this period—worried and confused. Don't give in.) After this period, say "Sit" once. If he obeys, praise him, or if you'd like, offer a treat. Repeat throughout the day at brief intervals. The key is not to reward your dog with affection unless he obeys you. As he responds more quickly, up the ante. Make him sit in three different spots before you give affection. Get closer to him. Over time, you should be able to enforce a command like *get off* without fear of attack.

    If your dog is a resource guarder, have him sit before putting down his food bowl. Your dog should sit promptly and without complaint. Half-hearted compliance is not acceptable. If your dominant dog refuses to sit, put the food dish away and try again in 20 minutes.

15. **If only one person in the home is the target of aggression, this work should be done by that person.** Remember that your whole family must share this effort. If one person is sneaking hugs, kisses, and soft words to the dog while the rest of you aren't looking, the entire program is doomed. It's like sneaking cookies when on a diet.

16. **Keep social-climbing dogs off the bed.** While some people have no problem sharing a bed with a dog, I don't recommend it. Even the nicest dogs won't let you get a good night's sleep. A dominant

dog may use the privilege to assert his position in the household.

17. **Manage playtime.** Human beings should initiate all play behavior with dominant-aggressive dogs, not the other way around. You decide when to start and stop games. The point is to encourage your dog to look to you as the source of all fun. If your dominant or aggressive dog brings you the ball without your asking for it, for example, just walk away. Play on your terms. With fear-aggressive dogs, on the other hand, it's a good idea to allow the dog to come to you because he will have his fears assuaged by your continued gentleness, and his stress levels will be reduced.

18. **Learn dog language.** Growling, for instance, can be a warning or threatening signal, but it can also be used in play. While the difference is always clear to dogs, human beings sometimes have trouble decoding it. A dog in play posture, wagging his tail and growling, is not usually threatening and should not be treated as such. However, the same growling and wagging combo can be a warning sign in a dog not in play posture. In other words, some aggressive behavior can mimic play behavior. Puppies who emit very deep, low growls are showing a level of aggression that is undesirable. (For more on canine body language, see sidebar "Smart Stuff: Dog Body Language.")

19. **Exercise your dog.** Sometimes increasing a dog's exercise helps head off aggression, partly because a tired dog may be too exhausted to bite and partly because exercise increases the level of serotonin in the brain. However, lots of aggressive dogs get plenty of exercise, so it is certainly not a panacea. Still, exercise is so beneficial in so many ways that it's silly not to try.

20. **Change the diet.** We know that serotonin affects mood and that this chemical is synthesized in the body from tryptophan, an essential amino acid found in meats and soybeans. A diet high in meat products like roasted chicken breast and turkey can substantially increase the level of tryptophan in your dog's system, making it easier for him to produce serotonin and help him stay calmer and stress-free. Some early studies have vindicated this approach. (Former theories about using a low-protein diet to control aggression do not work.)

21. **Teach bite inhibition.** Puppies who have not learned this essential skill from their littermates need you to be their teacher. The rule is: Dog teeth do not belong on human skin. If your puppy grabs your hand in play, cry out as if hurt and stop the game. (Don't pull away your hand, though, remove his teeth from it. If you pull away, his tendency will be to clamp down.) He will quickly learn that nipping leads to serious fun loss. Use a toy, never your hand, when playing with your puppy. (This is a preventive, not therapeutic, technique.)

IF ALL ELSE FAILS

If all else fails, you may have to consider euthanasia. There are rare cases where, after diligent search, no cause can be found for dangerous, aggressive behavior and thus no treatment program can be instituted. If your dog is a serious threat to others, you may have to consider this option for the safety of your friends and family—and to avoid a lawsuit.

Never hug or kiss an aggressive dog; he may interpret holding, hugging, and squeezing as an invasion of his space.

22. **Desensitize and countercondition.**
When aggression stems from fear (which is most of the time), a dog can be helped by a program of gradual, systematic desensitization and counterconditioning. The goal of such therapy is to reduce his hyper-reactivity, which can stimulate aggression. Desensitization means, as the word suggests, to make less sensitive and so reduce the exaggerated reactions your dog may have to ordinary stimuli. It is accomplished by gradually exposing him to "weaker" versions of whatever "sets him off." A less intense version of the stressor can be smaller, farther away, or appear more briefly than the normal stressor. In sensitization, the trainer very gradually increases the stimulus in intensity or frequency until the dog stops noticing it. Counterconditioning means providing a pleasant reward for a dog's association with a stressor. Giving a dog a treat when he sees the fearsome vacuum cleaner, for example, is an example.

23. **Try pharmacology.** Psychoactive drugs are most effective on dogs whose aggression is clearly fear-related. The neurotransmitter systems have many different receptors and enzymes that regulate the production and metabolism of psychoactive drugs, thus making medication a possible therapy for aggressive animals.

Aggression is accompanied by decreased serotonin in the brain. Drugs that work to keep serotonin levels where they should be include the SSRIs (selective serotonin reuptake inhibitors); also effective are the tricyclic antidepressants clomipramine and amitriptyline, although both can have side effects, as with any other medications. (These drugs should not be given to animals with seizure disorders.) Other choices include buspirone, an azapirone that enhances serotonin, and selegiline, a monoamine oxidase inhibitor (MAOI). These medications are by prescription only but are not expensive if they can be obtained in the generic form.

I want to emphasize that drug therapy for any behavioral problem is not a cure-all. Dogs vary in their responses, so a medication that may work for one won't work for another. In addition, most psychotropic drugs do not take full therapeutic effect for four to six weeks. There may also be changes in the neurotransmitter receptors that make the medication less beneficial over time, even if initial results are encouraging. Psychoactive drugs should be regarded only as short-term therapy used to facilitate training, and medical therapy should always be combined with training. Medications are not a replacement for training.

What Not to Do

What you don't do is always as important as what you do, and it's always critically important not to ruin good positive effects with a misguided action. One mistake on your part can set your dog's progress back for a long time.

1. **Ignore it.** Aggression will not disappear on its own; instead, it will escalate and broaden to include other situations unless you take decisive measures. This is because it has brought its own reward—stress relief.

2. **Punish your dog.** Punishment is a poor tool for handling aggression. Dogs associate punishment with the punisher, not with the behavior. Punishment may temporarily stop the behavior but will have no ongoing effect. Physically striking a dog, as well as such apparently benign punishments as leash popping, muzzles, alpha rolls, yelling, water squirting, and throwing things at a dog, serve one purpose only: They make a stressed, fearful dog even more anxious. (In particular, striking a dog anywhere near his head produces a biting or snapping reflex, the precise behavior you are trying to correct.) The same is true of choke collars, electric collars, and prong collars.

It is especially dangerous to apply punishment to "pre-bite" aggressive behavior, like growling. The dog may learn that his warning growls will be punished, so he may decide to skip that step and go right into biting. Alpha rolls and similar "dominance"-based corrections are of dubious value. While they sometimes appear to get results, the dog may simply redirect his aggressive behavior to a family member perceived as lower in rank. (This is sometimes called "behavioral

Forcing an aggressive a dog on his back puts him in a very vulnerable position and may trigger an attack.

fallout.") The misunderstanding that aggressive treatments work came about because they *seem* to work. Applying force may appear to make the behavior go away, but in reality it is still there, waiting for the moment the collar is removed or the screaming, jerking, and hitting stop. Sometimes a dog will cease his aggressive behavior when the punisher is out of the room but then take it out on an innocent bystander.

3. **Chain or tie up your dog.** Tying up a dog leaves him feeling vulnerable because it eliminates one of his natural options in the face of danger: running away. This is also why tied-up dogs tend to bark more than dogs left free to move away from danger. Immobilizing a fearful dog while a stranger enters his territory is an invitation to disaster. In her study, "Fatal Dog Attacks," Karen Delise found a close link between lethal aggression and the tying up of a dog, noting "Chaining a dog is arguably the single most dangerous condition in which to maintain a dog. Statistically, chained dogs are more dangerous than free-running packs of dogs." Additionally, dogs kept chained often have had little opportunity to bond with people or other dogs and have failed to learn how to behave nonaggressively.

4. **Use inappropriate body language.** Never hug or kiss an aggressive dog. Many dogs interpret holding, hugging, and squeezing as an invasion of their space at best and as an aggressive move on your part at worst. While the average domestic dog learns from puppyhood that your unaccountable desire to wrap your arms around him and squeeze is not meant as a threat, a stressed, undersocialized dog doesn't get it at all and may bite the hugger. Similarly, don't lean or hover over an aggressive dog. This is much the same as hugging. Stressed dogs regard leaning as an aggressive move, not as the sign of affection for which it may be intended.

   Never stare at a potentially aggressive dog. This is an age-old signal of aggression. Although most dogs accept a stare with nonchalance, a stressed or fearful dog may react differently. Even human beings respond negatively to stares, often with a "What the heck are you starin' at, Buddy?"

   Running away and screaming are very much like prey behavior and can trigger it in dogs with a strong predatory drive. Obviously, most adults aren't going to do this, but a child might. Also, yelling at your dog will only make him more stressed than ever, and the situation will just worsen.

5. **Roll your dog over on his back.** Forcing an aggressive a dog on his back puts him in a very vulnerable position. When your pet voluntarily rolls over for you to rub his belly, he is showing you that he trusts you. However, forcing a dog to roll over is another kettle of fish, so to speak. The dog will feel threatened and may attack. Dominance-based training developed this "alpha roll" because submissive wolves were seen rolling in front of an alpha. However, the difference is that the submissive wolf initiated the behavior—he wasn't forced into it.

6. **Forcefully extract something from a dog who is "guarding" it.** "Trading" with a dog or teaching him the *leave it* command will help. (See Chapter 4: Training Basics.) Be sure to reward him lavishly and promptly with a treat of greater value than the purloined item. In the same vein, never take away his food bowl during a guarding episode. This ploy merely serves to deepen the dog's conviction that he must protect his dinner at all costs.

7. **Play competitive games.** How about a good game of tug-of-war? Dog experts can't seem to make up their minds whether or not playing tug encourages aggressive behavior in a dog. It hasn't in my experience. My shyest and most submissive dog is the most dedicated tugger, and I have seen no evidence whatsoever that dogs can't distinguish between playful tugging and serious biting. However, if you own a dog who has displayed aggressive behavior in the past, common sense says not to reinforce it in any form. Play a cooperative game like fetch instead.

8. **Pass your problem dog over to a rescue or shelter without being totally honest about the dog's behavior.** Most nonkill shelters and rescues are not able to accept aggressive dogs into their adoption program for obvious reasons. However, some dog refuges will do so. In any case, it is dangerous and wrong to misrepresent your dog's character. Telling a shelter that you are giving up your dog because someone in the family is "allergic" to him when he has just bitten off your hand is unfair and dangerous.

TRAINING CHECKLIST

✓ Keep yourself and your family safe.
✓ Acknowledge the seriousness of the problem.
✓ Do not confront or challenge a dangerously aggressive dog.
✓ Be a strong leader.
✓ Reward friendly, cooperative, and submissive behavior; avoid yelling or physical punishment.
✓ Give your dog exercise, consistency, and a regular schedule.
✓ Get professional help.

Chapter 6

Aggression: Dog–Dog

Dog-on-dog aggression occurs when one dog takes aggressive exception to the behavior, or in some cases, the mere presence of another dog. In some cases, dogs object to strange dogs, while others nurse a grudge against a fellow dog in the household. Dog-on-dog aggression occurs with relative frequency in the dog world, and often, the offending dog is sweet as pie to human beings. Many times the objectionable dog is of the same sex, age, and size as the offender—but not always.

Within the same household, larger dogs are usually dominant over smaller ones.

In many cases, dog–dog aggression has its roots in a struggle for social promotion among other dogs in the home. Most, but not all, household dogs establish themselves into some sort of dominance hierarchy within the home. This order can be affected by the following factors:

- Size: Larger dogs are usually dominant over smaller ones.
- Length of residence: Earlier residents tend to be dominant over later-comers.
- Gender: Males are often dominant over females.
- Breed disposition: Terriers and dogs with a guarding or fighting heritage tend to be dominant over more easygoing breeds like hounds and setters.

However, this order is not etched in stone. When there is an upset in the family (e.g., death, divorce, new baby, new dog), stress increases and social hierarchies can be upset.

Dominance patterns can also be variable. One dog may be dominant most of the time, but another may take command under different circumstance or refuse to yield a particular toy or bed. One of my dogs is the boss inside the house but takes a backseat to another when outdoors. As they move into old age, senior dogs may yield their position of dominance to a younger dog. It is very natural for dominant dogs to occasionally reassert their dominance by posturing or even growling at the more submissive dog. Fighting that occurs in the absence of the owner suggests that a dominance hierarchy has not yet been established among the dogs.

It's well to remember that any dog of any breed may decide that he does not like:
- a specific individual (but may get on fine with others)
- dogs of the same sex
- smaller dogs
- larger dogs
- dogs of any breed other than its own (yes, dogs do know)

My rescue group once took in a dog who hated small, white, fuzzy dogs. He was fine with big, white, fuzzy dogs; small, white, shorthaired dogs; or small, black, fuzzy dogs. Somehow it was the combination of tininess, whiteness, and fuzziness that sent him completely over the edge.

Causes

Dog-on-dog aggression has as many causes as it has manifestations. It is among the most common and normal of "problem behaviors."

Medical Conditions

Many of the same medical problems that cause dogs to attack humans can also be factors in dog-on-dog aggression. See Chapter 5: Aggression: Human for details.

Wolf Heritage

- **Natural dominance structure.** Wolves have two interrelated ways of behaving: 1.) They form packs to hunt cooperatively, and 2.) they form dominance hierarchies to maintain social order. Most household dogs do not form a neatly organized, structured "pack," at least not like wolves, although some groups of household dogs do form dominance hierarchies. I don't consider a dominance hierarchy a pack because in a true pack, animals work together cooperatively to achieve a goal. Cooperative hunters like wolves, foxhounds, and hunting Beagles do this. Family dogs, not so much.

However, pack or no pack, many household dogs form a "dominance

Terriers—like this Bull Terrier—and dogs with a guarding or fighting heritage tend to be dominant over more easygoing breeds like hounds and setters.

hierarchy," as wolves do also, although in a household the "leader" will be a singleton alpha dog, not a bonded pair, which is how wolves operate. Wolves naturally form a hierarchical, single-sex dominance system; in other words, there is one dominance pyramid for males and another for females, with the oldest animals usually at the top and the youngest at the bottom. Cross-sex dominance systems are virtually nonexistent. In a wolf hierarchy, there is a dominant couple on top, with their offspring and perhaps a few other animals lower on the totem pole. Wild wolf packs not only have an alpha male but also a

Competition for owner attention can cause jealousy and animosity between two dogs.

second-ranking, or beta, male who is often the single most aggressive animal in the pack; however, he saves his aggression for the dominant male, whom he continually challenges. More than traces of this behavior can be found in today's domestic dog. The lowest-ranking wolves tend to be much more sociable both inside and outside the pack, a trait also seen in modern canines.

Although dogs in a family can often get along quite well and may even bond strongly, their primary relationship is almost always with their owners, not each other. (True pack dogs, on the other hand, bond more closely to each other and tend not to form a dominance hierarchy. Examples are found primarily in hunting pack dogs.)

- **Competition.** Attachment to an owner is an aspect of life that creates tension between dogs. They compete for the owner's goodwill and table scraps; they don't work cooperatively to get them. However, sometimes, when no clear dominance hierarchy has been established, one or more dogs may decide to apply for a "leadership" position (which may or may not be actually available).

SMART STUFF
Leader of the Pack

In the wild, wolves live in groups called packs. Jumbling up several unrelated dogs in a house does not automatically transform that group into a pack, with you as the pack leader. The entire "pack leader" concept is largely overblown, anyway. The whole idea got started in the 1940s, when studies were done on groups of captive wolves collected from various places that, when forced to live together, competed for status. And this is sort of what a modern multiple-dog household is like. But it is far from a natural situation. Wolves in the wild, according to L. David Mech, founder of the Minnesota-based International Wolf Center, live in nuclear families, in which the mother and father wolves are the pack ("family") leaders and their offspring's status is based on birth order. (Mech used to go along with the alpha dog theory, but closer study has altered his opinion.) There is very little competition in a natural wolf pack because youngsters naturally follow their parents' lead. They also have unlimited space in which to work out their relationships. The situation is very different in today's "multiple-dog" household. Multiple dogs, randomly and forcibly placed in "family units" with little room to maneuver, run, or hide are in a decidedly unnatural state. Their wolf heritage is of little help here. The unnaturalness of it all places them under a good deal of stress, which in itself can turn into aggression.

The German Shepherd Dog is just one specific breed that has been known to show aggression toward other dogs.

That can lead to fighting. While we adore the way our dogs can become attached to us, this same loving affection can lead to displays of resentment and jealousy (as well as separation anxiety, discussed in Chapter 19).

Even when a group of family dogs seems to form a peaceful dominance hierarchy with an "alpha" dog, that status is fluid and changes with circumstances and time. In my house, a Gordon Setter is the alpha dog inside but the Dalmatian mix pretty much runs things outside. Another dog seems to be in charge of the toys.

- **Prey drive.** Some cases of inter-dog aggression, such as an attack on a smaller dog by a larger one, may be simply a result of wolf-inherited natural prey drive. There is little that can be done about this other than relentless supervision; if both dogs are household members, one may have to be rehomed.

Breed Predilection and Genetics

Most dogs get along pretty well with each other, but in some breeds it's a stretch due to how they were bred and what they were bred for.

- **Bred for aggression.** Most terrier and pit bull-type breeds were actually bred to have a high degree of inter-dog aggression. They have inherited the wolf's exclusivity (its intense suspicion of strangers) but have also lost the wolf's aptitude for cooperative effort among its own. Aggressive-leaning breeds seem to be more apt to form linear hierarchies, but in social, democratically minded breeds, several animals may hold the same "rank."

Some kinds of terriers and mastiff-type dogs were once bred specifically as fighting dogs, and it is said that in times past, fights sometimes went on for days until one of the participants was dead. To some extent, bad relations between terriers is encouraged in the show ring, where entrants are frequently expected to "spar" with one another to show off their feistiness and courage. This is especially true at all-terrier shows. (Not every terrier breed is sparred, but most are.)

Specific breeds that may show aggression toward other dogs (this usually applies to two or more males) include:

- Akita
- Alaskan Malamute
- American Staffordshire Terrier (or "pit bull")
- Borzoi
- Boxer
- Chinese Shar-Pei
- Chow Chow
- Doberman Pinscher
- French Bulldog
- German Shepherd Dog
- Jack/Parson Russell Terrier
- Kerry Blue Terrier
- Poodle
- Scottish Terrier
- Staffordshire Bull Terrier (or "pit bull")

On the other hand, most pack hounds like Beagles tend to get along very well with others.

- **Lack of signaling.** Some dogs have been under selective breeding pressure that tends to suppress accurate communication of their intent to attack—thus, many attacks upon other dogs (or even people) by dogs of these breeds seem to come out of nowhere. Wolves tend to use certain well-defined signals to display dominance or status, such as standing stiffly across the forequarters of reclining subordinate wolves or grabbing an opponent's muzzle and forcing it to the ground. However, this kind of signaling is relatively rare in domestic dogs, with the exception of Huskies and similar ancient "wolf-like" breeds.

- **Competitive behavior.** Among dogs of the same litter, it has been observed that competitive behavior develops when the puppies are three to four weeks old, with pair-wise relationships becoming stable by about the eleventh week. During that time span, there is considerable fluidity, with some puppies moving from the top to the bottom of the order and back again within days. (This research was done with two completely different breeds—Border Collies and French Bulldogs—but the results were the same.) This fluidity has a practical, if somewhat disturbing, implication: The so-called puppy temperament tests, which are typically performed

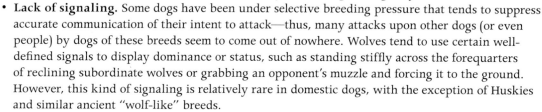

SMART STUFF

Basket Muzzles

Whenever you are dealing with a potentially dangerous situation and you are afraid for the safety of a dog or person, use a basket muzzle on the dog. This will prevent serious damage to anyone.

Too many dogs put into too small a space almost inevitably leads to squabbling.

well before the age of 11 weeks, are not reliable tests of future dominance. If these tests are to have any value, they should be conducted later, at around the 11-week mark.

Regardless of whether testing is performed before or after the eleventh week, rankings do change and altercations between dogs can develop. Some breeds, like Shetland Sheepdogs, tend to quarrel over space, while others, like Basenjis, argue more over food. In more social breeds, like hounds, an individual of either sex may end up dominant. In less social breeds, like terriers, the alpha is generally male. This is especially true when the males of the breed tend to be larger than the females.

Environmental Factors

Certain environmental factors can contribute to dog–dog aggression:

- **Lack of puppy socialization.** Like children, puppies need adequate socialization with their own kind to ensure that, as adults, they can be peaceful partners in a home. Unfortunately, many puppies are taken from their littermates too early to develop these skills, and this can ruin their social lives forever.
- **Crowding.** Too many dogs put into too small a space almost inevitably leads to squabbling. Dogs

need room to get away from one another, and a large number of dogs in a house is always a bad idea.

- **Owner miscues.** Owners who seem to fear or dislike other dogs pass on their feelings to their own dogs, whether they mean to or not.
- **Upsetting the pack hierarchy.** Owners who attempt to equalize things by giving special attention to the bottom dog in the household may be inviting the dominant dog to attack or may give false hope to the bottom dog. It's best to let the dogs sort things out for themselves (within reason).

What to Do

You can have a great effect on keeping the situation manageable if you will follow through and remain strong and in charge yourself.

1. **Take note(s).** Assess the level and kind of fighting in which your dogs are engaging. Some dogs fight only in the presence of their owners, in which case the fighting acts as a function of the way owners interact with them. Others are fine together as long as the owners are present but can't be trusted alone. Keep a log for a week or two, noting times, places, and specific circumstances associated with the behavior. If you take your dog to a trainer or veterinarian, she will need this information. Video-record the behavior if possible.

2. **Socialize your dogs.** Dogs who play together stay together, so it's up to you to provide plenty of opportunities for free and fun interaction between dogs. Most dogs don't enjoy fighting and are just waiting for you to provide the right conditions for them to make friends. Many kennel clubs provide "growl classes" to help owners learn to socialize loner dogs. You will probably never turn a loner dog into a social butterfly, but if you can stop a few fights, you will have come a long way.

Socializing your dogs can help prevent future fights.

3. **Train your dogs.** A trained dog is a

SMART STUFF

Should You Add a New Dog?

Before adding a new dog to your current mix, consider your reasons. It is generally not a good idea to get a second dog in the hopes of resolving the problems of the first dog. A second dog is not guaranteed to ensure that your first one gets more exercise or will be less lonely while you are at work. It may turn out that way, but believe me, there is no guarantee. In reality, adding a new dog is actually more likely to add tension and create problems than to solve them. In any case, do not add a new dog until the first dog is completely trained.

If you do decide to add a second dog, it is usually best to select one of the opposite sex of your first dog. Introduce the new dog slowly, on neutral, fenced ground if possible. Before the actual introduction takes place, make sure that each dog is thoroughly exercised. When it's time for the introduction to take place, the larger the area, the better. Many experts recommend keeping the new pair on leashes while introductions are being made. However, my many years of experience with rescued dogs suggests that this technique is likely to trigger aggression. Leashed dogs feel trapped and unable to flee, so tension mounts.

Rather than keeping hold of the leashes, drop them entirely. Allow both dogs plenty of room to get out of each other's way. Most will soon show interest by sniffing each other's rear (correct protocol in Dog Universe), and the pair will soon be playing or cheerfully ignoring each other. (For the first meeting, I would leave the leashes attached to the collars so that you can grab them if necessary.) If the dogs show persistent signs of aggression, you may have to rethink your decision to add another dog to the household.

responsive dog who will obey his owner rather than getting into a squabble. All dogs should respond to basic commands like *sit* and *come*. Also, take your dog to a Canine Good Citizen class, sponsored by the American Kennel Club (AKC). There, he will not only learn basic commands but also how to approach other dogs.

4. **Castrate your male dog.** Castration lowers the compulsion of male dogs to fight with each other. It is especially helpful in preventing fights among family dogs, totally curing about ten percent of them and substantially improving the behavior of the other ninety percent. When fights do occur, they are less serious. Females with puppies or in estrus can also be quite snappish with other dogs.

5. **Establish and reinforce a hierarchy.** This is no place to flaunt your predisposition toward equality for all. Most dogs haven't taken civics classes, and they approach life from a more primitive standpoint. If your dogs are fighting in your absence, it indicates that they haven't yet settled into an established hierarchy. It then becomes your job to help create one. If the dogs can't decide who is going to be top dog, you'll have to nudge them a little. The best criterion would be to think like this: "Okay, if push really comes to shove, would Buster beat Buddy or vice versa?" Then you back the winner proactively by feeding him first and giving him priority attention.

In addition, greet and pet the dominant dog first. This reinforces the natural hierarchy they have established and helps create a calmer, more peaceful atmosphere in the home. If the dogs fight only in your presence, you know that you are doing something to trigger the outburst. That something is probably not reinforcing the relationship that has already been established. So if the

Never put your dogs into a situation in which they have to compete for food or toys.

subordinate dog attempts to gain access to you by pushing aside the dominant one, give him the cold shoulder and interact with the dominant dog first. It seems mean, but you'll be happy with the results. The dogs too will experience less stress. If the lower-ranked dog continues to aggress the more dominant one, speak sharply to him. This works more often than you might think.

6. **Remove the triggers.** Never put your dogs into a situation in which they have to compete for food or toys. Dogs, even friendly ones, are not hardwired to share. If you do hand out toys or food, do it separately. If you are playing a throwing game with them, use two balls and throw them in opposite directions.

7. **Analyze body language.** A stiffened stance, laid-back ears, snarls, and a rigid upright tail may indicate that serious trouble is brewing. If you sense a problem, separate the dogs, not allowing any visual contact. When things have calmed down, try taking them for a brisk walk together.

8. **Limit your interactions with both dogs (short term).** Avoid all social contact, especially displays of affection with them. It is particularly important not to allow the "underdog" to sleep on your bed. This creates a false sense of safety in the underdog, and he will feel that you are giving him permission to challenge the dominant dog. The dominant dog will resent the favoritism and dislike the underdog even more, creating more tension. It is sometimes permissible to allow the dominant dog to sleep on the bed if the other dog sleeps in a different room. This generally works only if the underdog is a new dog and hasn't become accustomed to sleeping in any particular place.

9. **Desensitize your dogs.** Find that critical distance at which no stress is triggered and gradually work to bring the dogs closer together. Use a head halter for maximum control—you'll be able to turn the dog's head rather than putting pressure on his neck and raising his stress levels. Ask the aggressor to sit while the friendly, cooperating dog is brought into view and then out again. Ten such experiments make up one session. The next session should aim to bring the dogs even closer together. You may only be able to move a few inches (cm) closer a week. If your quarreling dogs are large or dangerous, get the help of an expert trainer.

10. **Take both dogs on leashed walks together.** This activity keeps their minds off their rivalry and makes a connection between good times and the other dog. But control your dogs if they

lunge while on walks. If your leashed dog exhibits aggressive behavior toward another dog, turn and walk away. If he quiets down, you can try approaching again, always using praise and treats if he does what is right and non-confrontational. This works more often than you might believe. In any case, it is unwise to allow a potentially dangerous situation to develop. If your dog is not unalterably dangerous, try this: Walk your dog behind the other dog. (Face-to-face meetings are the most confrontational.) Do this until your dog seems less anxious and stressed. Then start walking side by side, headed in the same direction. If all goes well, you can attempt face-to-face greetings.

11. **Introduce the dogs on "neutral ground."** That way you can control their interaction, at least to some extent. Let the dogs smell each other and get acquainted for at least ten minutes. Ask both dogs to sit and give them a treat. The idea is for them to associate the other dog with good things.

12. **Give each dog his own time and space.** Use some of the time you spend with each dog for fun and play, but spend some time on training too. This is a chance for you to practice your leadership skills and for your dogs to learn to obey you. When they respect you as a calm, consistent leader, less fighting will occur.

To help take their minds off their rivalry, take your dogs on leashed walks together.

While the use of a muzzle can eliminate the chance of real bodily harm, it should be used only as a last resort because it does nothing to defuse tension between two dogs.

13. **Avoid a provocative situation.** Sometimes nothing works. It's often possible for your dog-hating canine to enjoy life without coming into direct contact with other dogs. If your dog picks fights at dog parks, it's up to you to find an alternate way of exercising him: long walks, flying disk in the backyard, jogging, or any other activity that prevents your unleashed menace from attacking others.

14. **Consider progestin therapy.** For female "underdogs" in cases of female–female aggression, progestin therapy can help. This will encourage more submissive behavior on the part of the female dog.

What Not to Do

Success depends just as much on what you avoid as on what you accomplish.

1. **Punish the dogs.** As always, punishment simply increases fear and stress. This does nothing to solve the original problem and may cause the dog to redirect his aggression at the punisher, i.e., you.

2. **Interfere with an established hierarchy.** Forget equality. Dogs have their own culture and generally work out a dominance order among themselves. Unfortunately for household peace, humans sometimes try to assuage the "hurt feelings" of lower-ranked members by petting them and giving them extra attention. This does two bad things: It makes the dominant dog jealous and anxious to reassert his position, and it gives the lower-ranked dog the false hope that he can

WHEN ALL ELSE FAILS

If all else fails, consider reducing your number of dogs. Studies have shown that for every dog added to a household, the stress level of the resident dogs increases. If you have continual fighting among dogs that no amount of intervention and training can assuage, you may simply have to consider rehoming some of them to give everyone a chance at a more peaceful life.

achieve a higher position. To gain it, he may try to attack the more dominant, probably larger dog, and get seriously bitten in the process. It's up to dogs to establish their own hierarchy.

3. **Let seriously fighting dogs "sort it out" on their own.** Minor squabbles are usually self-limiting and need no interference, but continued or dangerous fighting must be stopped. For many dogs, once a fight has escalated into uncontrolled territory, the relationship between the two will never be the same again. Some people think that putting muzzles on the rival pair and letting them duke it out, so to speak, will yield a lasting peace. Not so. While the use of muzzles does eliminate the chance of real bodily harm, it does nothing to defuse tension between the pair. They will continue to be in a world of heightened excitement and stress. It also leads the subordinate dog to believe that he can safely confront the dominant dog. Muzzles should be used only as a last-ditch effort. Sometimes, after a fight, the dogs will never get along.

TRAINING CHECKLIST

✓ Establish and reinforce a hierarchy.
✓ Take your dogs to socialization and obedience classes.
✓ Castrate your male dogs.
✓ Make sure that all dogs get plenty of directed exercise.

Chapter 7

Begging

We all recognize a begging dog, even though he doesn't carry a cardboard sign. A begging dog sits, sometimes patiently, sometimes not, at your side, carefully watching every morsel of food that you consume. Occasionally, long strings of drool slide hopefully from his jaws, and every once in a while a low agonized moan escapes his lips.

Like other mammals, dogs are programmed to be hungry just about all the time. And because most of them have no coin collections or favorite television shows, eating occupies a goodly portion of their daily concerns.

Begging has an instinctive base, but its full-blown manifestation is a learned behavior, a behavior that is reinforced by a dog's owners (often unintentionally). And why not? Dogs are social beings and so are we. What is more natural and social than sharing a meal with a friend? In fact, in a positive light, begging can be looked at as a bonding experience with your dog. However, natural as it seems, food sharing creates a problem behavior—and depending on what you're feeding, possibly health risks as well. Grapes, onions, macadamia nuts, and chocolate can be toxic to dogs, and chips, cookies, and fatty meats aren't any better for them than they are for you. Also, obesity in pets has reached mammoth proportions. (Almost 50 percent of American dogs are overweight, and 15 percent are clinically obese.)

The begging habit is easiest to break by not letting it start in the first place. Dogs are intelligent—they easily figure out that begging works. It only takes one tiny morsel of food slipped surreptitiously under the table by a child convinced that she doesn't like carrots.

Even if your dog is not actually jumping and whining and pawing but only sitting and staring "mournfully" at you, this is still considered begging. Such dogs are subtler in their approach but no less earnest (and effective). It is even possible, although rather unlikely, that a dog whose begging is successful sees himself as moving up in the family hierarchy—and begging can turn into nudging and then demanding food.

Sharing food with your dog can actually have dangerous consequences, especially if he ingests something toxic, like chocolate.

Causes

In general, dogs beg because they want food or attention, but if we want to be scientific about this, we can break it down further.

Medical Conditions

If your previously well-behaved dog starts begging, there could be a medical reason for it.

- **Severe hunger.** One valid medical reason a dog might have for begging is severe malnourishment. I trust that this is not the case with your dog. In fact, it's probably the opposite situation, now isn't it? An ordinarily hungry dog should not be begging.
- **Malabsorption syndrome.** Some medical issues such as inflammatory bowel disease (IBD), cancers, or parasitical conditions exist in which dogs are not able to properly digest and metabolize their food, even though they continue to eat well. Such dogs are slowly starving and are, of course, are always hungry.
- **Medications.** Certain medications like prednisone make dogs hungry all the time. This could initiate begging for food.

In general, dogs beg because they want food or attention.

Wolf Heritage

- **Correct social behavior.** Dogs and wolves are social animals, and they see you, at least in some respects, as their leader. Ordinary dogs do not growl and threaten their owners for a slice of the pizza the way they might with another dog. They beg, the way a more submissive wolf might do to an alpha wolf. They do this by lowering their body posture and licking the muzzle of the senior or high-ranking wolf.
- **Family manners.** Young wolves beg their parents for food, and this behavior is encoded in your dog's genes. Wolf pups actually encourage their parents to regurgitate food by begging from them. Females confined to a den with nursing cubs will also beg their mates for food. Often, the male will comply without even being asked.

Breed Predilection and Genetics

Any dog can become a beggar, but some breeds have mastered that lean and hungry look even when they have just eaten.

- **Breeds tending toward obesity.** Breeds that tend toward obesity, like Beagles and Pugs, may be particularly adept at mastering "the look."
- **Breeds that drool.** Some breeds have added a prop to their lean and hungry look. Basset Hounds and Newfoundlands, for instance, are able to produce a long glob of drool while staring intently and sadly at your plate. Their strategy here is to make you lose your taste for your dinner and hand it over to them.

Environmental Factors

- **Weak-willed owners.** While all dogs have a natural instinct to beg, the behavior becomes ingrained only when you allow it. Dogs are smart enough not to persist in unrewarded behavior.
- **Occasional slipups, even unintended ones.** Food is so highly prized that giving in just once is enough of a reward to motivate the dog to continue to beg for many weeks. The "reward" does not have to be from you. Kids are primary culprits. On the old Art Linkletter Show segment, "Kids Say the Darndest Things," one child defined good manners in the following way: "Good manners are not throwing food under the table unless you know there is a dog under there." Unfortunately, accidentally dropping food on the floor acts an unintentional reward. Your dog probably doesn't care how it got there. However, smarter dogs do seem to recognize the contextual difference.

Never feed your dog from the table, which will just reinforce the begging behavior.

My dogs are not permitted to beg at dinner, but one of them lies quietly under the table ready to snatch up any mishandled tidbits.

What to Do

Unfortunately, the way to get a dog to stop an ingrained begging habit is going to take a lot of patience and persistence from you.

1. **Feed your dog his meals on a schedule.** When dogs eat regularly, they are less anxious about when they will be fed and thus feel less compelled to beg.
2. **Never feed your dog from the table.** Not ever. Not once. Giving into that look just one time will land you in a world of serious trouble. A single crumb is enough of a reward to keep your dog going back for seconds for the next six months, and I am not exaggerating.
3. **Feed your dog at the same time you eat.** That will take his attention from your plate to his, at least for about 90 seconds. Afterward, he should feel a little fuller and less inclined to beg.
4. **Feed your dog in his own spot.** Getting your dog in the habit of eating only in his own dining area may help reduce the impetus to beg.
5. **Build your dog's patience.** Instill patience in your dog when you give treats. Hold the treat in

Your dog should have his own special place where he eats his meals.

your hand but don't give it out until he sits, or better, lies down. Never respond to a whine or nudge, and don't hand out treats simply because your dog stares at the treat jar and starts barking at it. That's a mistake I've made.

6. **Be patient.** You and your dog will be in for a hard time. Dogs will not give up this highly rewarding habit easily. (It takes about 30 days for a dog to form a new habit.) Zero tolerance must be your policy. And for a while, things may get worse rather than better. Your dog will up the ante. If staring doesn't work, he may try whining. If you still hold out, he may start nudging. Taller dogs place their heads on the table. When that fails, they start pawing. If you give in at this stage, you are really in for trouble because you have successfully taught your dog that persistence and upping the ante pays off. Instead, continue to ignore the behavior or immediately remove your dog from the vicinity, and steadfastly ignore any barking or whining that may ensue. It will be painful, but keep telling yourself: "This is my own fault, this is my own fault."

What Not to Do

You probably already know what not to do because that's how you got into this mess in the first place. But I will spell it out.

IF ALL ELSE FAILS

When you are eating, remove your dog from the dining room or kitchen to a spot as far as reasonable from your own regular eating place. (This will work even better if you confine your own eating to a table.) This will help your dog understand that his spot is his and yours is yours. I know that you've tried explaining this verbally to him, but it won't work. This is a management technique rather than a cure, but over time it will extinguish the behavior.

1. **Give in.** Do not reward begging ever, ever, ever. If you've already failed here, you'll have to hang tough. Use an analogy. Let's say that your three-year-old demanded one of your martinis or some of the dog's kibble—you would never allow this! Nor would you allow your dog to eat grapes, chocolate, onions, or other toxic foods just because he wants them. In the same way, and in the interest of your mental health, don't give in to your dog. Eventually, he will cease his unrewarded behavior. But it won't happen overnight, and remember, you have only yourself to blame because you inadvertently reinforced the begging behavior in the first place.

2. **Give a begging dog your own food even when he's not begging.** If he knows he will never get it, he will be less inclined to beg for it. If you absolutely must feed your dog some of your food, wait until well after dinner and scrape it off your plate into his bowl. Or put it in the refrigerator and feed the following day. This is what I do in my house with healthy leftovers. Unless I get to them first.

TRAINING CHECKLIST

✓ Never give in to begging. Never.
✓ Feed your dog (including treats) on a regular schedule.
✓ Feed your dog in a regular spot.
✓ Do not punish a begging dog. It's your fault.

Chapter 8

Chasing and Predatory Behavior

Dogs come from wolves, and wolves make a living by running down and killing things. Some dogs are "activated" by sight, some by smell, and some even by hearing. (That squeaky toy touches deep roots in your pooch.) However, this natural behavior leads to all sorts of depressing results. Dogs break out from their yards and attempt to run down cars or are run over by cars; others chase or may even kill the family cat or a smaller dog.

The act of chasing things releases adrenalin in a dog's system that feels great and encourages him to continue the activity.

Causes

Chasing is a completely natural behavior. Its roots go deep into the doggy psyche.

Medical Conditions

Chasing things is a sign of health, rather than the reverse. In fact, the very act of chasing things releases adrenalin in a dog's system that feels great and encourages him to continue the activity. That's hard to compete with.

Wolf Heritage

Wolves are born to run and chase. Chasing wildlife, even for domestic dogs, is an instinctual natural response that can't be extinguished easily. As mentioned earlier, this is the normal predatory process, which consists of the following phases:

- orient to prey (actively seek out appropriate prey)
- get a fix ("eye") on the prey
- stalk the prey
- chase the prey
- grab/bite the prey
- kill the prey
- tear apart and eat the prey

Breed Predilection and Genetics

Not all dogs display the full chase/attack/kill pattern of a wolf. For most dogs, gaps appear in the sequence.

- **Heelers.** Heelers, such as Australian Cattle Dogs and Texas Heelers, will chase and grab/bite.
- **Pointers.** Pointers, such as German Shorthaired Pointers and German Wirehaired Pointers, will orient, eye, and grab/bite only.
- **Retrievers.** Retrievers, like Labrador Retrievers and Golden Retrievers, will orient and grab/bite the prey. They won't stalk or chase it. Retrievers of all kinds, as well as Jack/Parson Russell Terriers, Rottweilers, and Border Collies, also seem to top the cat-chasing ranks of dogs. Also included in this category are northern, prick-eared, spitz-type breeds.
- **Sighthounds.** These dogs, like Greyhounds, Whippets, and Rhodesian Ridgebacks, exhibit all phases of the pattern except for "eyeing" it. Sighthounds have a powerfully developed predatory drive, and larger members of the group are extremely prone not only to chasing things in general but to running down and killing small animals, including the family cat.
- **Sheepherders.** Sheepherding breeds like Collies, German Shepherd Dogs, Shetland Sheepdogs, Border Collies, and Australian Shepherds are known as stock-protecting dogs and have a very attenuated prey drive. This is critical; otherwise they would devour their charges.

The same is true for sheepherding breeds like Corgis, who routinely chase and nip their charges

Sighthounds, like this Rhodesian Ridgeback, are prone to chasing behavior.

but who are programmed to stop the attack short of seriously injuring them. (Experts say that the latter stages—grab and kill—of the typical wolf hunting pattern have been suppressed.)

- **Terriers.** Terriers, such as the American Pit Bull Terrier, tend to have a powerful predatory drive that includes other dogs, cats, rabbits, and in some cases, human beings.

Only the truly wild dog or wolf goes through the entire predatory cycle unhindered. In many breeds, certain of these traits are "hypertrophied," or strongly emphasized, like the eye of the Border Collie or Pointer or the grab/bite of the retriever. Some dogs can even get "stuck" in one phase of the pattern. Pointers are intentionally "stuck" in the eye phase and are not supposed to go chasing after the prey. Only when the game is shot are they allowed to grab-bite it (gently). Sometimes a dog gets "stuck" accidentally in a phase and is not able to proceed to the next step for which he was bred. Breeders who breed working dogs remove these dogs from their program.

Although in many dogs chase instinct and predatory behavior are profoundly linked, for others this is not the case. Plenty of dogs will chase a cat but never hurt it, while others may ambush and kill a small animal. Often, the predatory drive is triggered when the prey animal runs.

Most dogs never exhibit kill behavior to animals they grow up with; my Irish Setter, Flannery, would chase all cats except the two she knew from puppyhood. Livestock guardians like the Great Pyrenees are brought up with sheep, and their prey drive toward them is suppressed. However, they may go after rabbits or other animals they don't consider part of their flock. They are also territorially aggressive and will fiercely protect their flocks from intruders, human or otherwise. Some of them barely tolerate their owners. Having said this, I should note that in actual practice, very few livestock guardians ever get into a fight with predators because wolves and coyotes have

Certain environmental factors contribute to chasing behavior, such as a moving object.

the good sense to stay away from a bunch of hysterically barking dogs. They'll look for something easier or wait until they think that the dogs have gone home to dinner. It is not to a wolf's advantage to fight over prey, even against a much smaller animal.

One thing is certain: Dogs do not chase something because they are hungry, and keeping your pooch well fed will do nothing to allay his chasing habit. It is an ingrained behavior.

Environmental Factors

Certain environmental factors contribute to chasing and predatory behavior.

- **Moving objects.** In many cases, the chase cue is simply a quickly moving object—ball, child, or car.
- **Running away.** Running in the opposite direction while screaming joyfully and flopping

SMART STUFF
Fenced Yards
One reason that it is critical to keep your dog safe in a fenced yard is that when a group of dogs get together, it will almost certainly gang up and go on a chasing or perhaps even killing spree. This is called, in fancy language, "socially facilitated predation."

on the ground when "caught" is a delightful reward for most dogs. Kids do it all the time. Throwing balls and flying disks also accentuate a dog's natural chase instinct.

- **Small animals.** The mere presence of a small animal like a squirrel is enough to drive many dogs crazy—even if it freezes in an attempt to escape notice.

What to Do

Because this behavior is so largely genetic, managing the situation is a safer option than trying to "train" your dog out of it.

1. **Manage the environment.** Chasing is a deep-seated behavior that is not easily controlled. Any dog who follows the predatory sequence completely to aggression and killing prey is never trustworthy around the chosen item. Ever. If your dog has ever attacked a cat, for example, he should not be trusted with them again. It's up to you to keep your cat safe by strict segregation or the rehoming of one of your pets. If your dog is a car chaser, the reasonable solution is a fenced yard at least 6 feet (2 m) high for bigger dogs. The best option may be a wooden

or covered fence that will reduce outside stimuli. For determined chasers, make sure that the fence is buried several inches (cm) into the ground.

2. **Start training early.** Some kinds of predatory chasing behavior can be avoided if started early enough. Properly socialized working foxhounds, for example, display strong aggression toward foxes but not chickens. This behavior has been developed by careful breeders who place their young foxhounds with "puppy-walkers"—farmers who have chickens. Because hounds do not typically develop hunting behavior until after this "farm animal socialization period," the dogs can be safely trusted around chickens even while running through a yard full of them while after a fox.

   At the same time, training your dog to come at your command is a must. Practice doing this at odd times—not just when you want him to come in for dinner. Reward him with intermittent high-value treats so that he'll be inclined to race to your side. However, because some temptations are too strong to resist, you will always need to keep your chase- or escape-prone dog in a secure fenced yard. Equally important commands are *leave it* or *drop it*. (See Chapter 4: Training Basics.) If you own a dog with a strong prey drive, you just can't trust him around small pets. If you have a cat chaser, leash your dog. Let the leash dangle from the collar, but the instant he charges after the cat, step on the leash and bring the dog to a screeching halt.

If your dog is a car chaser, the reasonable solution is a fenced yard.

3. **Choose your breed carefully.** Toy breeds and many Working and Non-Sporting Group dogs are not known to be major chasers. Terriers and all hounds and sporting breeds may be characterized by a high prey drive.

4. **Introduce dogs and cats slowly.** Cats and dogs are not natural friends and do not form a natural family. They have to become accustomed to each other. Be watchful and always provide your cat

To prevent cat chasing, introduce them slowly and always make sure that the cat has an escape route.

with a quick escape route. (You can put a baby gate between rooms, leaving the gate high enough for the cat to make a clean getaway.) Give your dog special attention when the cat is around. Soon, he will associate the cat with good things. However, this is not a foolproof method. Dog who chase cats don't "hate" them; they just regard them as prey. If you suspect that your dog is a cat chaser, you cannot leave them alone together. If either of them gets overstimulated (cats will run and dogs will chase), a problem could occur.

5. **Timing.** Timing is important. Many common prey animals are most active at dawn and dusk. Keep your dog indoors during those hours.

What Not to Do

In most cases, chasing can only be redirected, so it's important to use good sense in addressing the problem.

WHEN ALL ELSE FAILS

Because this behavior is difficult, if not impossible, to extinguish, you may have to rehome your dog or persecuted pet. Pets do not enjoy being chased by large barking dogs (even if they mean no harm), and it is cruel to subject them to it.

1. **Punish your dog.** Punishment only creates stress, which can be displaced to the prey object. This includes tying the carcass of, say, a dead chicken to your dog's neck in the vain hope that he'll stop chasing them. Get a grip. Nothing could be nastier or less effective.
2. **Trust your dog.** Once a chaser, always a chaser. You can't fix this—you can only manage it. Never allow your dog to run free outside your yard.

TRAINING CHECKLIST

✓ Keep your dog on a leash when in the presence of possible "prey."

✓ Introduce dogs and cats carefully.

✓ Teach your dog to follow basic obedience commands, like *come* and *leave it*.

Chapter 9

Chewing

It's a gnawing concern, isn't it? Dogs are chewers by nature, and you must expect that all young dogs (at least up to the age of six months) need to chew. Because dogs don't have hands, mouthing objects is one way they learn about the world. (Babies do the same thing, even though they have hands.) Chewing is also essential to the teething process; it's called "setting the teeth" and occurs when the adult teeth are coming in at seven to eight months. Chewing is, of course, a prelude to eating, and while some dogs may chew nicely on their toy bone for hours, others take the next programmed step in the eating process—which is to dissect the object and perhaps to swallow it, with potentially dire results.

Because dogs don't have hands, mouthing objects is one way they learn about the world.

Most dogs are not indiscriminate chewers, however. In other words, they won't eat just anything. Indeed, they have decided preferences: brand-new things, expensive things, irreplaceable things, and dangerous things, not necessarily in that order. Designated toys may rank rather low down on the desirability scale. They also love items that smell like you, especially your shoes and underwear.

If your dog is chewing from separation anxiety, please see Chapter 19.

Causes

Although you may never know exactly why your dog has suddenly decided to eat the sofa, it may comfort you to know that there is no shortage of possible reasons:

Medical Conditions

A variety of medical conditions can cause chewing, including the following:

- **Oral pain.** If a previously nonchewing dog starts munching down on household items, he may be experiencing pain in his oral cavity. Chewing makes gums feel better. Look for broken teeth, red or swollen gums, or sores. If you notice anything odd, check with your veterinarian.
- **Teething.** Teething is an uncomfortable process, and chewing seems to alleviate some of the pain

and pressure in a puppy's gums.

- **Malabsorption.** Medical conditions that lead to malabsorption, like inflammatory bowel disease (IBD), may also contribute to inappropriate chewing.
- **Dietary deficiency (usually mineral).** It is possible, although frankly not very likely, that your dog is engaging in this kind of behavior to make up for something lacking in his diet.

Wolf Heritage

Wolves have big chewing teeth, of course, which they can use to crush the bones of caribou and the like. And while wolves seldom chew up a person's home, those individuals who own wolf-hybrids are often treated to a world of destruction when they come home after work.

Breed Predilection and Genetics

I don't want to get into any trouble here. Just like all dogs can bite, all can chew and destroy things. So I'm punting this to www.homeownersinsurance.org to get its opinion (and statistics) based on a 2008 UK survey of 3,000 dog owners and the amount of money spent to repair their pets' damage. Here are its top ten chewers:

1. Basset Hound
2. Beagle
3. Boxer
4. Dachshund
5. Bulldog
6. English Setter
7. Whippet
8. Mastiff
9. Chihuahua
10. Great Dane

One thing is for certain: This is much more a matter of individual predilection than of breeding. Most of the damage came from puppies, but 14 percent of owners said that the damage continued throughout the dog's life.

These statistics are just generalizations. None of my many Basset Hounds altogether were half as destructive as a certain Gordon Setter I own. The stats come from a single survey—and let's face it—one breed had to come out on top. I daresay a second survey might turn up completely different results.

Environmental Factors

The local environment is not the only target of a dog's destructive chewing; it can also be the cause of them. The following factors can play a role:

- **Poor training.** Many dogs were simply not taught as puppies what was permissible to chew and what wasn't.
- **Boredom.** Dogs are highly intelligent animals who need things to do. If left alone all day, even when they don't suffer separation anxiety, they will create their own fun—with your precious items.

- **Attention seeking.** If your dog starts to chew on inappropriate objects while in your presence, it may be a bid for your attention.
- **Loneliness.** Lonely dogs may chew things as a means of self-soothing. When things get bad enough, lonely chewing can turn into full-blown separation anxiety. How can you tell the difference? If your dog begins to chew the instant you leave the house, it's a good bet he's suffering from separation anxiety. (See Chapter 19: Separation Anxiety.) If a couple of hours go by, he is probably simply bored or lonely (but not to the point of separation anxiety—yet).
- **Lack of exercise.** Dogs need to work off their energy somehow. It's up to you whether your pet lies on the sofa all day or goes for brisk walks around the neighborhood.
- **Food left on or near furniture.** Your neglectful housekeeping is setting a perfect storm for destructive chewing. Your dog may start by licking up peanut butter and jelly leftovers and

One study has identified the Basset Hound as the number-one chewer.

finish by eating the couch.

- **Emotional stress in the family.** Dogs are sensitive and respond to family crises by going a little off-kilter themselves. Dogs in this class usually self-correct when things calm down a bit.
- **Presence of mice or other critters in the walls or floors.** If your dog targets walls or floors, it's possible they contain something you'd rather wish wasn't in there. In this case, it won't matter if you're home or not for the behavior to occur.

What to Do

One of the most important things to keep in mind with a persistent chewer is that chewing is almost universal in puppies. As dogs get older, they tend to chew less.

1. **Take note(s).** Assess the level and kind of chewing behavior in which your dog is engaging. Keep a log for a week or two, noting times, places, and specific circumstances associated with the behavior. It is particularly important to know if the behavior takes place only in your absence or in the presence or absence of other dogs. If you need to take your dog to a trainer or veterinarian, she will need this information. If you can video-record this information, so much the better. Dogs who chew up furniture only when alone may be bored or anxious. On the other hand, dogs who go after only

THE EXPERT SAYS

Dog trainer Kathy Diamond Davis writes: "During the most rampant chewing stage, it pays to bring in new and interesting toys frequently. Some people rotate the toys to keep them interesting. Just remember to keep an assortment of textures available to the dog at all times. This will likely mean that you have some toys in every room where you and the dog spend time."

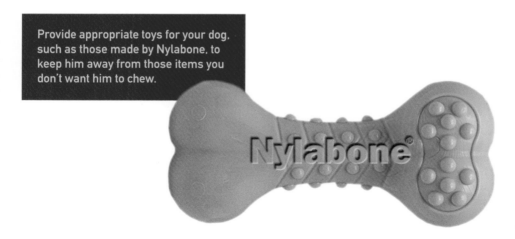

Provide appropriate toys for your dog, such as those made by Nylabone, to keep him away from those items you don't want him to chew.

garbage or other "edible" material are generally motivated by greed, not emotional difficulties.

2. **Supervise your dog.** Your dog should be supervised, at least until he understands the rules about chewing. A watched dog is a less destructive dog. Never leave a chewer alone in a vulnerable room.

3. **Provide appropriate toys.** Your first line of defense is to provide your dog with interactive toys. Look for toys that are fun, safe, strong, and easy to clean, like the ones Nylabone makes. For many dogs, the best toys are combined with food. In the wild world, after all, play behavior is often intricately connected with hunting skills. In the past, dogs had to work for their food. This exercised their minds and their bodies at the same time, which is why one great group of toys is food puzzle toys.

The most important thing to remember is that your dog's toys should be clearly differentiated in his mind from important household objects like shoes. This explains why you should never give a dog an old shoe to play with; he can't be expected to understand the difference between a "good shoe" and a piece of junk.

To help your dog know which items are appropriate to chew, try this. Lay out a number of appropriate chew toys and one forbidden object like a shoe. Say "Get your toy!" When he selects a correct item, praise him. If he gets the shoe instead, say "No" in a firm voice and ask him again to get a toy. Don't try to yank the offending toy away—make a trade for a better toy or a dog biscuit. Over time, you can increase the number of inappropriate items and still be confident that your dog will select which toys are his. If you do this consistently, you can gradually decrease the number of chew toys while increasing the number of inappropriate items. In about two weeks, you should be able to lay out one chew toy and nine inappropriate items, and your dog should consistently pick up only the correct chew toy.

4. **Put away your things.** An obvious but often overlooked method of keeping your valuables safe is

Teething dogs will feel better if they are given ice cubes or a frozen washcloth to chew.

Supervise your dog until he understands the rules about chewing.

to keep them where your dog can't get to them. Put away scarves, shoes, and books in their proper places. Also, close doors, which will at least limit the amount of damage your dog can do.

5. **Try ice.** Teething dogs will feel better if they are given ice cubes or a frozen washcloth to chew on—it's comforting to the mouth and satisfies the urge to chew at the same time.

6. **Keep your chewer safe.** Tape down electrical cords, and keep window cords out of reach. It is amazing what dogs will eat—some have devoured entire t-shirts and even knives. Dog-proofing seems tedious, but look at it as a way to improve your housekeeping skills.

7. **Give your dog sufficient, human-assisted exercise.** Regular periods of vigorous exercise (not just on the weekends) are necessary for the health and happiness of high-energy dogs. If you can't provide this yourself, consider a dog walker or doggy day care. It's important that this activity be scheduled regularly. When your dog can rely on exercise at a certain time, he is much less likely to be destructive in the home. If you aren't as mobile as you'd like to be, even a game of fetch will help.

8. **If you're snowed in, have a broken leg, or it's too darned hot to go out, indoor games can keep your dog occupied and exercised.** Use the hallway for fetch, play hide-and-seek, or just

Exercise and your attention will help alleviate your dog's boredom.

practice some simple obedience moves. Your attention and simple physical movement will do much to relieve boredom.

9. **Use aversive sprays on furniture.** You can buy commercial products that taste bad but are safe for use on upholstered items—and they won't harm your dog. You can also make your own spray with a cayenne pepper base. Once your dog gets the idea that furniture tastes bad, he'll probably stop. However, in other cases, you may have to reapply at intervals.

10. **Check for vermin.** Wall and floor chewers may be trying to tell you something. It never hurts to check.

11. **Offer a mineral supplement.** If you suspect that your dog's diet is lacking in an important mineral, you can offer a supplement. However, don't do so without your vet's approval.

What Not to Do

Remember that chewing comes naturally to dogs, so use restraint, patience, and good sense in addressing the problem.

1. **Punish or scold your dog after the fact.** Chewing is a normal activity, especially for puppies, and should not be suppressed. It just needs to be redirected in an appropriate direction. Remember to keep tempting "toys" out of reach.

2. **Offer inappropriate toys.** Dogs seem to have an unnatural affinity for smelly socks, pantyhose, and underwear. Apparently, they smell irresistibly of you. All of them can be not only chewed but swallowed, sometimes with disastrous results, particularly in the case of pantyhose, which can actually slice the intestines. And while some dogs love cow hooves, they are the number-one cause of tooth breakage. Choose safe chew toys made specifically for your dog.

3. **Keep your dog outside.** This will simply redirect his inappropriate behavior to digging or barking without doing anything to fix the real problem.

WHEN ALL ELSE FAILS

When all else fails, crate or contain your dog. Crating will keep him out of trouble, but this is a stopgap method only to be used in conjunction with the training detailed in this chapter. You can also keep your dog confined to certain "safe" rooms in the house to reduce the chances of his getting into trouble.

TRAINING CHECKLIST

✓ Understand why your dog is chewing.

✓ Supervise your dog.

✓ Make sure that your dog gets sufficient exercise.

✓ Give him a variety of tough, interactive toys.

✓ Keep dangerous and valuable items out of reach.

Chapter 10

Dietary Indiscretions

Like people, dogs have taste buds, although they don't have as many of them as we do, and some of them appear to be in the throat. Maybe that's why they gulp everything. Most of the taste buds dogs do have are the so-called Group A receptors, which respond to sugars, including artificial sweeteners and amino acids. (Unfortunately, some artificial sweeteners, like xylitol, found in certain low-calorie chewing gums, are deadly to dogs.)

Some dogs will eat anything they can get into their mouths, like grass.

Fructose and sucrose seem to arouse the taste buds most. This makes complete sense in the wild because wild dogs must often dine on what they can scavenge, which could mean sweet items like berries. However, the substance that really gets canine taste buds rocking is amino acids, explaining the dog's preference for meat. Unlike herbivores, dogs don't crave salt because they get more than enough of it in their natural, meat-filled diets.

In any case, dogs eat far more than the kibble regularly assigned to them. Some eat pretty much anything they can get into their mouths, including feces, grass, dead animals, and even rocks. Fortunately, one of the glories of being a dog is their storied ability to vomit up things that don't agree with them. Recently, a Labrador Retriever and a Basset Hound teamed up to unearth (Lab) and devour (Basset) no less than 31 nails. With timely veterinary intervention, the Basset recovered from the ordeal. My own Basset, Clovis, consumed a spatula, which subsequently needed surgical intervention.

One particular form of dietary indiscretion is coprophagia, the eating of feces. Not only is this a disgusting habit, it's also dangerous. Dogs can contract parasites, but if they eat the stools of a large animal like a horse that was recently wormed, they can also be poisoned. (Keep in mind that coprophagia is to some extent a natural behavior—mother dogs eat the feces of their offspring to

SMART STUFF

Dangerous Foods

Whether you give in to his begging or he finds the stuff on his own, plenty of people foods can make your dog very sick. These include:

- Alcohol. Alcohol is a poison. In low doses, it makes people feel pleasantly high or woozy; in larger amounts, it kills. It has precisely the same effect on dogs, but it doesn't take much to kill them. Signs of alcohol poisoning include vomiting, breathing difficulty, and in severe cases, coma and death.

- Chocolate. Chocolate products contain substances called methylxanthines that can cause vomiting in small doses and death if ingested in larger quantities. (Coffee and caffeine have similarly dangerous chemicals.) The darker the chocolate, the more toxic it is. For smaller breeds, 1/2 ounce of baking chocolate can be lethal, while a larger dog might survive eating 4 to 8 ounces. Never take a chance—keep chocolate well out of your dog's reach.

- Grapes and raisins. No one knows the reason, but grapes and raisins (as few as seven) can cause renal failure in dogs.

- Macadamia nuts. These tasty treats cause weakness, overheating, and vomiting, and in some cases, temporary hind leg paralysis in dogs.

- Xylitol. This artificial sweetener is found in some sugarless gums and candy. In dogs, it causes a rapid drop in blood sugar or even liver failure.

Certain ornamental plants, both indoors and out, are equally likely to cause trouble. These include azaleas and rhododendrons (vomiting and diarrhea, even death in severe cases); tulips and daffodils (the bulbs can cause stomach and heart problems); and sago palms (the seeds can cause liver failure). Although most dogs ignore these things, adventurous puppies are not as judicious.

Dogs who eat nonfood items on a regular basis suffer from a condition called pica.

keep the den area clean.) Coprophagia can occur in several forms: autocoprophagia (eating one's own feces), intraspecific coprophagia (eating the feces of other dogs), and interspecific coprophagia (in which dogs eat cat poop, deer droppings, and the like). Some dogs practice all three kinds at once. Autocoprophagia has been noted in both submissive and dominant dogs. The submissive dog might be trying to conceal his presence, while the dominant one may just not want anyone stealing anything of his.

Dogs who eat nonfood items on a regular basis suffer from a condition called pica, which can be disturbing and dangerous. Dogs (or people) with pica are compelled to eat almost anything they come upon, although large amounts of clay or chalk seem to be favorites.

In any case, dogs, even otherwise healthy ones, seem to be especially fond of the following harmful items. (Perhaps all dogs have some degree of pica.):

- **Something organic (like a dead animal or feces of any variety).** While animal carcasses are unsightly, dogs usually manage to consume them without permanent damage. Remember, they are scavengers by profession. It's usually okay to just keep an eye on your dog for two or three days.

If he becomes lethargic or seems sick, call your vet.

- **Toxic materials.** If your dog ingests something that you know is toxic, like zinc pennies or other heavy metals, call your vet right away or contact the Animal Poison Control Center at (888) 426-4435. Experts are available to answer questions and provide guidance 24 hours a day for a consultation fee.
- **Sticks, strings, balls, and rocks.** Call your vet for immediate assistance. These things can block or perforate the stomach or intestine.
- **Grass.** About 80 percent of dogs love to eat grass, especially long-bladed grass. Then they vomit because they lack the enzyme to digest it. No one knows why dogs eat grass, but it doesn't seem to do any harm. It's possible your dog may just be hungry, in which case it's a good idea to feed smaller, more frequent meals. Perhaps it is an ancient way of purging the body, but the behavior still remains a mystery. If your dog is an inveterate grass eater, lay off the fertilizer. That's a lot worse than grass for dogs.

Like all mammals, wolves are genetically designed to be hungry all the time.

Causes

Dogs naturally eat anything they can get their mouths around, but serious cases can have causes that extend to disease and breed predilection.

Medical Conditions

While most cases of dietary indiscretion are not medically based, this can certainly be a factor.

- **Malabsorption disorder.** A malabsorption disorder, like exocrine pancreatic deficiency, can lead to dietary indiscretions. Apparently, the deoxycholic acid in the waste has a beneficial effect.
- **Other diseases.** Other diseases, including thyroid disorders, diabetes mellitus, and Cushing's disease, cause an increase in appetite or malabsorption and may account for the problem.
- **Medications.** Certain medications, especially steroids, also cause an appetite increase that may result in your dog eating things he shouldn't.
- **Mineral imbalance.** While this is unlikely, it is possible, as may be the case with some kinds of pica.
- **Excessive carbs.** Carbohydrates are not a large part of a dog's natural diet. Feeding too many of them can throw his whole system out of whack, which can in turn lead to abnormal eating patterns.
- **Obsessive-compulsive disorder.** In rare cases, a problem like coprophagia may be a compulsive disorder.

If your dog eats something like string. call the vet because it can block the stomach or intestine.

Wolf Heritage

Dogs and wolves share the same basic anatomical and physiological design, so it makes sense that many dog eating habits come from their forebears.

- **Basic mammalian design.**

Like all mammals, wolves are genetically designed to be hungry all the time. This makes complete sense in the wild. Most hunting expeditions are not successful, and if a wolf waited until he was weak and ravenous to search for food, he might die before he found any. Although wolves today are preferentially predators rather than scavengers, scavenging seems to have been an important element in the wolf-to-dog transition. It seems safe to say therefore that there is a genetic predilection for this behavior in dogs.

- **Preference.** Some dogs just like the taste of the things they shouldn't be eating, like grass or feces. No one knows exactly why this is, but since it appears in almost every dog at least sometimes, it is assumed that this is part of the genetic package they have inherited from wolves.

All domestic dog relatives display a great deal of adaptability in their eating habits, a practice that has stood them well over the centuries.

Breed Predilection and Genetics

Too much dietary indiscretion, of course, may lead to obesity. And obesity is a particular problem in (starting with the smaller breeds and working up):

- Cairn Terriers
- Dachshunds
- Scottish Terriers
- Cavalier King Charles Spaniels
- Beagles
- Cocker Spaniels
- Basset Hounds
- Labrador Retrievers
- Golden Retrievers
- Rottweilers
- Bernese Mountain Dogs
- Newfoundlands
- Saint Bernards

I have a suspicion that the same breeds most prone to obesity are the same breeds most likely to commit dietary indiscretions. I can't prove it, but it seems like common sense.

Environmental Factors

Although environmental control is not the sole answer, you can certainly manage your dog's environment sufficiently to prevent the worst indiscretions.

- **Hunger.** Your dog may just be plain hungry, and dumpster diving is a natural remedy. As a result, dogs on a diet may be more likely to engage in dietary indiscretions.
- **Attention-seeking behavior.** In some cases, coprophagia and other dietary indiscretions may simply be an attempt to get attention, even if the attention is negative.

SMART STUFF

Food Palatability Tests

Labrador Retrievers and Beagles aren't allowed to participate in dog food palatability tests because they will literally eat anything. Pack hounds in general seem predisposed to gobbling up anything in sight; perhaps this is because they were traditionally kept in large groups and fed out of troughs—it was every hound for himself. I can't account for the Labrador's voraciousness; maybe some of them just take after their owners.

Too much dietary indiscretion may lead to obesity, particularly in breeds like the Rottweiler.

Restrict your dog's access to trash if he has the habit of eating everything in sight.

- **Scolding during a housetraining accident.** Yelling at your dog for having a housetraining accident may cause him to eat the evidence in the future.
- **Boredom.** People raid the refrigerator when they are bored. Dogs eat their poop or perhaps other nonfood items for the same reason.
- **Doing clean-up duty.** If your dog is tied up outside or confined to a small area, he may simply be trying to neaten it up a little by disposing of the trash. Mother dogs eat the feces of their young to keep the den clean, so he's acting on instinct.

What to Do

If your dog has a habit of eating everything in sight, you need to be proactive.

Dogs on a diet may be more likely to engage in dietary indiscretions because they're hungry.

1. **Get a vet check.** In rare cases, the cause may be medical. (See section "Medical Conditions.")

2. **Restrict your dog's access to trash.** If your dog gobbles anything in sight on a regular basis, you'll have to be vigilant and manage the situation. Reduce the problem by picking up the yard and keeping your dog on a leash. We had to lock up our trash cans to keep Clovis from tipping them over.

3. **Supply your dog with healthy food.** Nutritious low-calorie, high-fiber treats like carrots, canned pumpkin, or broccoli may curb his urge to go dumpster diving.

4. **Eliminate table scraps.** While I generally have no objection to feeding healthy table food to dogs, those who commit dietary indiscretions are probably reinforced by them.

5. **Increase the number of meals.** Feed three or four meals a day to encourage your dog to feel fuller and lessen his desire to eat garbage and worse. Feed a high-quality diet with sufficient animal-based protein.

6. **Help your dog lead a fuller life.** Most dogs who eat nonfood items on a regular basis are kept confined in kennels or have a history of this type of confinement. By supplying your dog with plenty of attention and offering lots of exercise, you can help keep his mind on other things.

7. **Clean up dog waste as soon as possible.** Even the most coprophagic of dogs will fail in their quest if you diligently clean up his potty area.

8. **Try commercial products.** For dogs with coprophagia, certain natural products will supposedly make their feces taste awful. Of course, this technique only helps if the dog eats his own feces.

IF ALL ELSE FAILS

If all else fails, try a home remedy. Some people swear by meat tenderizers, crushed pineapple, B-complex vitamins, glutamic acid, monosodium glutamate, and sauerkraut. I have no idea whether these things actually work, but it probably won't hurt to try.

What Not To Do

It's difficult to eradicate this behavior, but there are certain things you should never do in your efforts.

1. **Punish or scold your dog.** If he is eating inappropriate items to get your attention, you're inadvertently rewarding him, albeit with negative attention. If he's actually sick, you're just being mean and should take him to the vet.

2. **Pick up stools in your dog's presence.** If you can help it, don't clean up after your dog while he's watching. That simply encourages his interest in his waste. He'll figure that you're as fascinated as he is with his production.

TRAINING CHECKLIST

✓ Feed your dog a healthy diet.
✓ Restrict his access to trash and dog waste.
✓ Give your dog plenty of exercise.

Chapter 11

Digging

Digging is a natural behavior, but humans don't like it. It turns yards into minefields, gets dirt all over the place, and provides dogs with escape routes into the great and dangerous outdoors.

"**B**ut keep the wolf far thence that's foe to men/For with his nails he'll dig them up again," wrote the playwright John Webster (c. 1580–1634). Although one hopes that you needn't worry about the family dog digging up dead bodies in the backyard, this behavior can be annoying. Not all dogs dig, but those who do dig a lot. Digging can turn a pleasant backyard retreat in a muddy, ugly minefield within hours.

Causes

The causes of digging may seem obvious, but sometimes you'll have to dig a little deeper yourself to uncover them (pun intended).

Medical Conditions

- **Your dog is too hot.** Dogs cannot sweat effectively to cool themselves off. (Their major sweat glands are between their paw pads.) Digging a nest in the cool earth makes a pleasant retreat from the burning rays of summer.
- **Your dog is too cold.** The earth retains both heat and cold longer than the ambient air. In the winter, digging a "den" serves to protect your dog somewhat from the elements.
- **Your dog has an obsessive-compulsive disorder.** This is not a common manifestation of the disease, but it can occur.
- **Your dog has separation anxiety or thunderphobia.** If the digging occurs only when your dog is separated from you or if he is outside during a thunderstorm, this is a likely explanation.

Wolf Heritage

Wolf heritage has a lot to do with why you have a digger on your hands.

- **Nest making.** In the wild, wolves dig in the earth to make nests for their young but seldom at other times.
- **Hormones.** Although earlier studies suggested that den digging might be a function of reproductive hormones, such as progesterone or estrogen, other research indicates instead that increased prolactin (a hormone, secreted by the pituitary gland, that is related to milk production) in spring elicits or mediates den-digging behavior. Sometimes, a wolf works on the project alone; at other times, the whole pack joins in.
- **Protection from the elements.** Wolves also dig to protect themselves from heat or cold but nothing as elaborate as a den.

Breed Predilection and Genetics

Most dogs may resort to digging for one reason or

Your dog may be digging to cool himself—the earth makes a pleasant retreat from the hot sun.

another, but the following types are especially predisposed to engage in the behavior.

- **Northern breeds.** Northern breeds like Siberian Huskies and Alaskan Malamutes probably "remember" the bitter nights of their homeland, and their heavy coats make them miserable in the summer.
- **Terriers.** The word "terrier" literally means "earther." Terriers are genetically hardwired to dig for vermin, and they have the skills and temperament to do so. Dachshunds can also be counted as terriers for this purpose.
- **Heavily coated dogs.** The blazing heat of summer encourages all heavily coated dogs to dig to cool themselves.
- **Black dogs.** Black absorbs heat, and black-coated dogs suffer from heat more than pale-coated dogs, making them more apt to dig.
- **Snub-nosed breeds.** These dogs have trouble breathing when the weather is too warm; they may resort to digging to cool themselves.
- **Hounds.** Hounds that are bred to go into dens after rabbits may extend their digging exploits to other theaters of operation.

Northern breeds tend to dig more than some other breeds because their heavy coats make them miserable in warm summer climes.

Environmental Factors

The following environmental factors may encourage your dog to dig:

- **Boredom.** Dogs confined to the yard for long stretches may amuse themselves with construction projects. However, they seldom get any further than digging the foundation.
- **Enticing smells.** Some fertilizers, like manure, smell great to dogs, just inviting them to dig deeper and envelop themselves in the enticing aroma.
- **Bone burying.** Dogs who are given bones, or in some cases, toys may wish to secrete them in a special place for later use.
- **Vermin hunting.** My Basset Hound Mugwump was an inveterate hunter of moles. She could hear them scurrying along their underground mole paths and would dig them out with delighted fury. Then she would eat them.
- **Desire to escape.** If your dog persistently digs near the fence line, you can surmise that he's planning a trip. Even though we had five fenced-in acres, one of my dogs was always trying to get away. He would sneak off in the woods and dig for a while, then come back nonchalantly. It might take him several days, but eventually he'd get under the fence and leave. We could never let

him out of our sight. Maybe your dog is looking for a mate or just wants to tour the neighborhood. Maybe he is terrified of something. (Many dogs panic in a thunderstorm and apparently think that if they leave the yard, they will also get away from the thunder.) If this sounds like your digger, see Chapter 12: Escaping and Wandering, for more tips.

- **Trying to get inside.** Dogs who dig by the house consistently may be lonely and are signaling their desire to come inside.

What to Do

Although digging is a natural behavior, it can be controlled and redirected.

1. **Supervise your dog.** You can't alter his behavior after it has happened, so don't allow your digging dog outside unless you're watching him. This is especially critical if he is trying to escape the yard.
2. **Exercise him.** A couple of hours of vigorous exercise every day decreases boredom and reduces the urge to dig.
3. **Provide interactive toys.** Chew toys, like those made by Nylabone, and food puzzle toys distract many dogs sufficiently to keep their minds off digging. Rotate them frequently to reduce boredom.

THE EXPERT SAYS

My good friend and dog trainer, Laura Hussey, from Atlanta, Georgia, says "Why do dogs dig? Because it's fun! So if you want your dog to stop digging you will have to provide an alternative that is just as much fun (at least for the dog). If you expect that you can tell your dog, 'No, no, bad dog!' and have him go out in the yard and not dig just to please you, then you will be sadly disappointed. Digging provides exercise and mental stimulation, and those needs must be met in some other way or your dog will either continue to dig or be a very unhappy dog (and possibly a very neurotic one, too)."

A great chew toy may distract your dog sufficiently to keep his mind off digging.

If your dog is digging because he's hot, offer him a small pool in the shade.

4. **Throw away the toy.** There is some evidence that dogs are likely to bury the toys they like least. They don't want them—but they don't want another dog to have them either. Save your dog the worry and chuck the toy away yourself.

5. **Bring him inside.** If your dog is digging not for recreation or to hunt moles but to keep comfortable, bring him inside. Heavily coated breeds benefit from a summer haircut. It is a myth that the fur of such dogs keeps them "comfortable" in the summer. It does not. The same is obviously true for dogs who are trying to make a cozy nest for themselves by making an earth den. Your own den is the best den for such dogs. Bring him in.

6. **Redirect his behavior.** Because digging is a natural behavior, one approach is to control it rather than attempt to eliminate it. You might select a particular, inconspicuous part of the lawn to designate as a "safe" digging area, or you can even construct a digging pit of your own, filled with a mix of sand and dirt. Using sand will help keep it well drained, an important consideration. To entice Fido to actually use the preferred spot, bury some toys and treats in it and let him watch you whoop it up "finding" them yourself and tossing around your newly discovered treasures. Your dog will want to join in. However, until he is firmly established in the new behavior—and this may take a couple of weeks—don't let him play in the yard without your

direct supervision. If he starts digging in an undesirable spot, patiently redirect him to the place you have chosen.

7. **Salt the digging spot with small rocks.** Dogs don't like that.
8. **Offer hot dogs a cool pool in the shade.** They will love it!

What Not to Do

Keep remembering how natural this behavior is. All natural behavior is difficult to extinguish, even when it is annoying and destructive.

1. **Punish your dog.** Digging is a natural behavior and should be redirected instead.
2. **Ignore the behavior.** If it bothers you or if it puts your dog in danger, you need to take active steps to redirect it.
3. **Let your dog watch you dig in the yard.** He may copy the behavior.

TRAINING CHECKLIST

✓ Give your dog plenty of exercise.
✓ Don't leave your dog outside alone for extensive periods.
✓ Redirect digging behavior.

Chapter 12

Escaping and Wandering

Dogs like to be "free." If they had their way, most of them would walk out the door in the morning, spend the day visiting neighborhood dogs and humans, scavenge garbage cans, chase local cats, dig up people's gardens, and return home sometime around dinner (if they could remember where home was after such an exciting day). In fact, during the Dark Ages (i.e., the time of my childhood), that's pretty much how most dogs lived their lives. It was also the reason why so many of them were hit by cars, caught in traps, tortured by mean children, and attacked by bigger dogs.

Wanderers by nature, many dogs would try to escape from their fenced yards if it were possible.

Fortunately, all of this has changed. Local laws and refined sensibilities have made us aware of the desirability—indeed, the necessity—of keeping our dogs safe at home. However, most dogs haven't agreed to the new rules. Most of them will slip out of the yard whenever a gate is inadvertently left open, and more enterprising pooches will make conscious and continued efforts to break down, dig under, or climb over a fence, or in some other way subvert their owner's will in this critical matter.

Dogs with thunderphobia kept outside or dogs with separation anxiety are desperate to escape their enclosures to find human companionship. My Basset Hound Ruby was in our yard one day when a thunderstorm blew in from nowhere. Before I could get outside to put her in the house, she had wrenched the gate open with her teeth (something she has never done before or since) and hightailed it down the road to take refuge with a friendly neighbor.

Like begging, this incredibly self-rewarding behavior is reinforced very powerfully after even one success. It really goes to a dog's head. Apparently, freedom is so satisfying among some dogs that they will try harder and harder to escape. Prevention is really the best medicine.

Causes

Although lupine heritage is the most common cause of running off, other factors, in particular breed type, also play an important role.

Medical Conditions

Escaping and wandering are natural behaviors and are almost never the result of a medical problem.

Wolf Heritage

It's in the genes, all right. Internationally known wolf expert L. David Mech reported that one Alaskan wolf pack covered 5,000 square miles (8,047 km) or more territory in six weeks. That's about half the size of the state of Maryland! In other words, your dog's "natural" roaming range is considerably larger than your backyard.

- **Instinct.** The escaping dog is not trying to "run away." He is simply following his instincts. If there is a female in heat in the region, intact males have a further impetus for their behavior. And females looking for a mate will wander far in search of one.
- **Loneliness.** Lonely but friendly dogs may be interested in searching for canine or human company and seek the attention of children or other dogs.
- **Fear.** Dogs are naturally programmed to try to escape a frightening situation.

SMART STUFF
The Flight Instinct Period

The critical period for developing an escape habit is between four and eight months old—the so-called "flight instinct period." If a dog gets loose during this time and has a positive experience, it's practically impossible to make him forget it; the memory of this joyful time is permanently imprinted.

Breed Predilection and Genetics

Some breeds are definitely hardwired to run off and can never be let off leash. They include:

- **Siberian Huskies.** These dogs are genetically programmed to run. This is one reason why they make such great sled dogs. (Contrary to popular belief, it isn't the pulling that gets them so excited; it's the act of running. They'd gladly run off without the sled if they could, but if they have to drag it also to gain a few hours of running time, so be it.)
- **Hounds of all types.** Hounds are independent types who are genetically programmed to follow their eyes or noses. They expect

Lonely but friendly dogs may be interested in searching for canine or human company.

Hounds of all types are hardwired to run off and so can never be let off leash in an unenclosed area.

you to keep up with them. They don't need your help in finding game and would probably be just as happy if you weren't following behind them.

Retrievers of all sorts and guard dogs, like Dobermans Pinschers, on the other hand, are less likely to stray. Retrievers are bred to work with their owners and can't do their "job" without them. Guard dogs are programmed to stay home and guard the property. Their strong territorial instincts make it less likely for them to forsake it.

Environmental Factors

But breeding isn't everything—surrounding factors also play a role.

- **Mistreatment at home.** Obviously, dogs who are abused at home have an incentive to try their luck elsewhere. While not as smart as cats about this, many dogs will try to escape a desperate situation.
- **Bad situation at home.** This is a little different than the previous bullet point. Even though a dog may not be abused, he could find something about his home situation unpleasant, such as too many other dogs, screaming kids, a lack of companionship, and so on.
- **Sexual allurements elsewhere.** Unneutered animals are naturally programmed to find a mate and are remarkably adept at doing so.
- **Lack of exercise.** Dogs need both mental and physical exercise. If they don't get it, they will create their own.
- **Poor fencing.** Inadequate fencing just invites a dog to leave. They don't especially hate their

homes, but an open road is a temptation too great to pass up. Almost all dogs will leave home, even if only briefly, to investigate the neighborhood if allowed to.

What to Do

With all but the most determined escape artists, it's fairly easy to keep your dog at home.

1. **Take note(s).** Assess the level and kind of the behavior. Keep a log for a week or two, noting times, places, and specific circumstances associated with the escaping behavior. If you need to take your dog to a trainer or veterinarian, she will need this information. It's important to understand why the escaping occurs. The longer the behavior has persisted, the harder it will be to extinguish. If it occurs as result of noise phobia or separation anxiety, those conditions must be treated as the primary problem.

2. **Contain your dog.** Assuming that your dog's wanderlust is not due to anxiety but is born from a natural desire to see the world, better

If your dog must stay in his crate or alone in the yard for extended periods, make his enclosure as attractive and entertaining as possible.

Train your dog to sit and wait before you open any door.

containment is your best option. Fences need to be higher, deeper, trickier, and stronger. For diggers, you may have to add underground metal stakes every foot (.5 m) or so, and climbers may require a wire addition or "roof" at the top of the fence set at a 90-degree angle. There is also something called a "coyote roller," originally designed to keep coyotes out but that serve well at keeping your dog in. You can make one by running some wire through sections of PVC pipe and hanging them as a sort of roll-bar. When your dog tries to climb the fence, he will be foiled.

Take every care when letting your dog in or out of his enclosure, perhaps by adding a "decompression area" for added security. With this design, the dog must get through two gates before he is truly "free." All gates should have dog-proof latches and self-closing springs.

3. **Enrich his environment.** If your dog must stay in his crate or alone in the yard for extended periods, make his enclosure as attractive and entertaining as possible with food puzzles and other entertaining, interactive toys. If his enclosure is quite large, you may decide to put less food in his dish and "hide" some around the yard, thus encouraging him to use his energy trying to find it rather than getting away. He should also have a shelter or "safe place" in the yard into which he can retreat if something scares him.

4. **Neuter your dog.** Neutering reduces the urge to roam in about 90 percent of cases, although it does not eliminate it. Unneutered animals have a biological mandate to mate, and they will do whatever they can to fulfill it.

5. **Consider adding a new dog.** Some dogs enjoy the company of another dog so much that it reduces their wanderlust. (This tactic will not work on dogs with separation anxiety or phobias, however.)

6. **Protect your dog.** A new device on the market is a wireless dog collar. The collar will send text messages or e-mails to you if your dog escapes the yard. It can also be set to allow continuous tracking, a wonderful idea for hikers and hunters, whose dogs might be off lead for extended periods.

7. **Supervise your dog.** Some dogs have chewed their way through chain link fences, broken down doors, and climbed 10-foot (3-m) fences. In cases of these accomplished Houdini dogs, your only recourse may be to constantly supervise him and send him to a dog sitter when you can't.

8. **Train your dog.** Teach him to "sit" and "wait" before you open any door. (To teach *sit*, see Chapter 4: Training Basics. For the *wait* command, have your dog sit and say "Wait," holding up your hand in a "stop" position. Use a leash if necessary. Then give a release word and drop your hand. Your dog should catch on quickly.)

9. **Attach a radio collar or special dog-friendly GPS device to your dog.** That way, if he escapes, you can at least find him more easily.

What Not to Do

Because escaping and wandering are natural behaviors, you should neither enforce them nor punish your dog for engaging in them.

1. **Punish your dog.** Scolding or striking a dog who has wandered off does nothing to convince him that he has anything to stay around for. He'll just try harder to escape next time. He will also assume that he is being punished for coming to you rather than for escaping.

2. **Reward your dog.** While you don't want to punish your dog, don't make the opposite mistake either. It's tempting, after having captured your errant dog, to fling your arms around him and praise him for returning or allowing himself to be caught, but that may act in his mind as a reward for wandering. It's probably best to seem indifferent to his return, even while you nonchalantly change the combination lock on the gate.

3. **Install an electronic fence.** They simply will not work on a determined escape artist.

Chapter 13

Housetraining Problems

Dogs generate about 4 billion gallons (15,141,647,136 l) of urine and millions of tons of poop every year. Not all of it ends up in your house, although I grant it certainly seems like that sometimes.

U rination in the dog world is more than simply emptying the bladder. It serves many functions: It can declare dominance or submission, and it is a calling card that reveals all kinds of information to curious canine passersby, including the health, sex, and status of the previous urinators. But for humans, dog urination can be fraught with problems. When not performed according to our expectations, we end up with soaked floors, stained rugs, and dead spots on the lawn.

Housetraining is both simpler and more complex than it sounds. It's simpler because we are not actually teaching the dog new habits; dogs instinctively do not soil their "den area." A wolf or wild dog's natural predilection is to be clean—to leave his den area unsullied by waste. Feces contain parasites that can reinfect if they are left anywhere near where the animal eats, and even urine, although naturally sterile, leaves a moisture buildup conducive to mold. Newborn puppies, in fact, only urinate and defecate when being cleaned by the mother dog, an excellent if unappealing way to keep the den clean. What we are trying to do is get the dog to understand that his "den" is the whole house and perhaps even part of the yard.

For humans, indoor dog urination can be fraught with problems, including soaked floors and stained rugs.

Causes

Wolves are naturally housetrained, so to speak, but in the dog world, a lot of circumstances can prevent or disrupt this desirable habit.

Medical Conditions

If your previously housetrained dog becomes incontinent, it is critical to have medical causes checked out first, as your dog may be suffering from something serious.

Urinary and fecal incontinence are different problems and may have different medical causes.

Urinary incontinence can be caused by any of these medical conditions:

- **Urinary tract infections.** Female dogs especially are prone to urinary tract infections, which make urinary continence difficult or impossible.
- **Urinary cystitis.** This is an inflammation of the urinary bladder. It can be caused by bacteria, bladder stones, tumors, or a number of other things.
- **Hormone-responsive incontinence.** Hormone-responsive incontinence is the most common medical cause for urinary incontinence in middle-aged and older females. The same condition can occur in young females and older neutered males but is less frequent. In females, the problem is a deficiency of estrogen; in males, it is a deficiency in testosterone. Both of these hormones help maintain the muscle tone of the urethral sphincter; when they go, so does your dog's control of his or her bladder. This kind of incontinence is akin to human bedwetting, occurring most often when the dog sleeps.
- **Neurogenic incontinence.** This condition occurs when something interferes with the nerves that control the bladder. This "something" can include spinal cord injuries, infections, tumors, and certain inherited conditions. When there is a problem in the bladder's nerve supply, it can't contract; instead, it continues to fill until it just can't hold any more. At that point, it starts to leak urine, and the dog constantly dribbles. There is a test called a cystometrogram (CMG) that measures how forcefully the bladder contracts in response to the introduction of fluid into it through a catheter. The results not only confirm the condition but may also point to the source of the problem.

- **Overdistension of the bladder.** This kind of incontinence is caused by a partially obstructed bladder. The obstruction is often bladder stones, but a tumor or a stricture is also a possibility. This condition may look like neurogenic incontinence, but the nerve supply to the bladder is undamaged.
- **Excitement urination.** Young dogs have weak, underdeveloped sphincter muscles. This fact, coupled with their boundless joy in seeing you again after a "long" of absence of 15 minutes or so, may result in a "leak."
- **Side effects of certain medications.** Some medications increase a dog's thirst and hence contribute to a need to urinate. If the dog is confined for a long time, things just naturally spill over.

    Fecal incontinence may be caused by any of these medical conditions:

- **Diarrhea-producing illnesses.** Enteritis, pancreatitis, colitis, cancer, inflammatory bowel disease (IBD), internal parasites, or any other disease that produces diarrhea could cause fecal incontinence. If you suspect that your previously housetrained dog is sick, get a vet checkup immediately.
- **Side effects from medications.** Any medication that produces diarrhea as a side effect may also produce fecal incontinence.
- **Food allergies, intolerance, or improper diet.** Any of these can result in diarrhea and consequent fecal incontinence.
- **Loss of sphincter tone in the muscles that cause defecation.** This is a condition that occurs with age and may trigger fecal incontinence during excitement, play, or even coughing. Eventually, all control may be lost.
- **Neurological problems like a spinal tumor or herniated disk.** Either of these can cause spinal compression, which injures certain nerves.
- **Misaligned vertebrae.** This could result from too much jumping or rough play.
- **Old age.** Over time, the sphincter muscle just seems to wear out.

Excitement urination can occur in dogs who express joy at greeting their owners upon their return home.

Old age can be one cause of incontinence.

Both fecal and urinary incontinence may be triggered by:

- **Canine cognitive disorder (CCD).** CCD is a medical problem of elderly dogs and is similar to Alzheimer's disease in human beings. The disease manifests itself by various behavioral changes, including loss of housetraining skills.
- **Arthritis or hip dysplasia.** Dogs with arthritis may find it so painful to move from their bed to the toilet area that they soil in the house, even though they don't want to. This condition can also cause urinary incontinence.

Wolf Heritage

Wolves are thrifty creatures, and they have a found a use for urination that goes beyond simple elimination.

- **Marking.** Like dogs, wolves are markers, and leaving their calling card is an important part of pack life. In fact, a wolf can decipher the details of an odor a dozen times more accurately than a dog can. In addition, urine is not as threatening to canine health as feces are, and it seems "naturally" easier to teach a dog fecal continence than urinary continence. (Of course, dogs need to defecate much less often than they need to urinate.) Unfortunately, marking is one of the more difficult behaviors to deal with. On the other hand, male dogs are unlikely to mark inside their own homes unless they feel competitive pressure from another male dog in the family. Females mark very rarely, although a dominant female may occasionally urinate over the urination of a previous dog, a kind of "so there" statement.

- **Submissive urination.** In the wild, submissive wolves exhibit this behavior but with approval rather than dismay from their superiors. It is a signal given to the dominant pack member that means "You have nothing to fear from me." It is most common in puppies and rescued dogs, with the "recipients" of the offering being human family members. The amount of urine passed is small.

Breed Predilection and Genetics

Some dog breeds, for reason of both anatomy and physiology, seem prone to difficulties in this department.

- **Smaller breeds (and puppies).** These dogs have smaller bladders and hence have less ability to "hold it" than older or bigger dogs.
- **"Low-hanging" dogs.** Dogs like Bassets are more prone to urinary tract infections. The important parts are just too close to the ground.
- **Terrier breeds.** Terriers, who tend to be inter-dog aggressive, seem to be more inclined to mark than other breeds.
- **Pack dogs.** Pack dogs, like Beagles, seem difficult to housetrain, according to my own experience and that of other owners. No one knows why, but my guess is that in former times they were

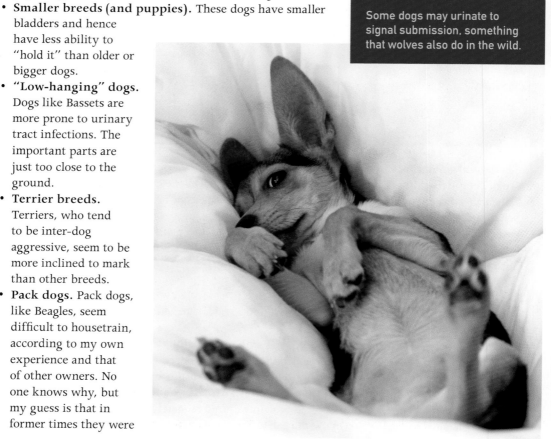

Some dogs may urinate to signal submission, something that wolves also do in the wild.

usually kept outside in large kennels rather than in or near homes. Nobody cared where they eliminated.

- **Male dogs.** Regardless of the breed, female dogs prove easier to housetrain (as a rule) than males. Again, no one is sure why, but it is reasonable to assume that because females don't mark, they are less apt to get mixed up about the purpose of urinating. They have no essential interest in peeing in the house.

Environmental Factors

A confused or inconstant environment definitely contributes to housetraining difficulties.

- **Nervousness or overexcitement.** Nervous dogs often exhibit submissive urination during periods of stress. Dogs do not make messes to spite their owners. Their leavings are the products of stress. They may make messes on the bed when you are gone because they are lonely, and that's the place your odor is strongest.
- **Separation anxiety.** Separation anxiety is a common cause of inappropriate urination. If you suspect that this is the problem, see Chapter 19.
- **Lack of supervision.** Most dogs give signs that they need to eliminate, but some owners are not sharp enough to pick up on them. These signs include going to the door, circling, whining, pawing, or looking "pained."
- **Unrealistic expectations.** Everyone has a limit. Sometimes owners expect their dogs to "hold it" for eight or ten hours. They wouldn't do that to themselves! In fact, forcing a dog to hold it for too long can lead to bladder stones.
- **Past trauma.** Some dogs, especially rescued dogs, have been confined in kennels for extended periods without the opportunity to relieve themselves. This essentially forces them to go against their own instinct and soil their "dens."
- **No clue.** Some rescued dogs who have lived outside in their previous lives simply don't understand that the house is off-limits, and they need to be taught how to eliminate outdoors.
- **Territory marking.** Male dogs, especially intact ones, have a habit of staking out their territory—especially when that territory is novel to them. It's a Y-chromosome competition type of thing.

What to Do

Housetraining problems are very common, but with good observation, patience, and consistency, they can be solved.

1. **Take note(s).** Assess the level and kind of soiling. Keep a journal, noting times, places, and

Most dogs give signs that they need to eliminate, such as going to the door.

specific circumstances associated with the behavior. If you need to take your dog to a trainer or veterinarian, she will need this information. When did the incontinence start? What is the consistency, color, and frequency of the stool or urine? Are there accompanying signs like gas or bloating? If it's bloody, smells horrible (worse than regular poop), or continues for more than a day, call your vet.

2. **See your vet.** Dogs with urinary tract infections need a course of antibiotics. There are also medical treatments for dogs with worms. Colitis and pancreatitis can be treated with anti-inflammatory drugs. Some dogs with spinal problems seem to respond well to treatment by a veterinary chiropractor. Females with hormone-responsive incontinence can be treated in two ways: Your vet may choose to prescribe phenylpropanolamine, a drug that increases the tone of the urethral sphincter (it can make some dogs "hyper," however), while another choice is diethylstilbestrol or estrogen (although this drug has been linked to bone marrow suppression). Incontinent males may be treated with testosterone or phenylpropanolamine.

Dogs with CCD may benefit from a medication called selegiline hydrochloride. The same medication is used in people to treat Parkinson's disease, Alzheimer's disease, and Cushing's disease. Dogs with overextension of the bladder are treated by removing the obstruction. In some cases, an indwelling catheter may have to be applied until muscular tone is regained. Neurogenic incontinence can be difficult to treat. The most effective course is usually long-term catheterization and antibiotics to combat any infections that may arise. Dogs with fecal incontinence may benefit from an antidiarrheal medication.

3. **Neuter your dog.** Both male and female dogs can mark. Males should be neutered; this simple surgery will eliminate or markedly (excuse the pun) improve the behavior. Even if your dog is an adult and has been marking a long time, neutering will help. Treat the marking dog just as you would a puppy who needs housetraining. Do not punish the dog. Remember that dogs tend to

associate punishment with the person wielding it—not with the behavior itself! Get his attention quickly by clapping your hands and taking him outside. (He doesn't really need to "go," but you're reinforcing the idea that elimination of any kind is not allowed in the house.) Females who tend to mark (and there are a few) may also benefit from spaying.

4. **Take your dog out more frequently.** This is especially important after a meal, play session, or doggy nap. Go out with him to ensure that he goes, and praise and reward him for doing so.

5. **Change his diet.** Dietary problems may respond to feeding several small meals rather than one large one. Feed on a regular schedule. Try switching to a high-fiber food that can produce bulkier (more solid) stools by absorbing stool water. Change foods gradually over several weeks to reduce the possibility of bloating and gas from the unaccustomed fiber. Other dogs respond better to a more highly digestible, low-residue food.

6. **Consider doggy day care or a dog walker.** Everyone, human and canine, has a limit to how long he can "hold it." It is cruel, unhealthy, and unfair to expect your dog to wait hour after hour to eliminate. You don't! If the problem is simply that your dog is over his limit, you need to take action. Small dogs and puppies have smaller bladders that just can't hold as much urine. This is not a "dog problem" but a human one. If you can get your dog into a doggy day care or hire a dog walker, the problem will solve itself. If not, and you own a smaller dog, you might be able to take advantage of various doggy litter pans on the market. Some of them claim to imitate real grass and are odor resistant. When your dog pees on the

If your dog is having housetraining accidents indoors, try taking him out more often and reward him when he goes.

Dog trainer and rescue dog behavior consultant Sandy Getz says, "Dog doors are great. But unless your dog has a modicum of housetraining to begin with, just installing a dog door will not help. In addition, some dogs are afraid of dog doors and need to be taught to use them."

tray, the urine trickles down in a collection tray that holds up to 1 gallon (4 l) of fluid.

7. **Try a doggy doorbell.** If you are simply missing your dog's signals, try attaching a "doggy doorbell" to the doorknob. You can make your own (simply a collection of jingly bells) or purchase a pet doorbell set, complete with training manual.

8. **Reward correct habits.** Too often, we forget to compliment our dogs (and each other) for good behavior. Dogs respond well to rewards and poorly to punishment, so this should be a no-brainer.

9. **Make a schedule.** Many centuries ago, the Greek philosopher Aristotle taught us that virtues are an acquired habit. Nowhere are the Philosopher's words more apt than in the matter of canine elimination. Virtue is truly acquired by regular habit. In housetraining, good habits result from a regular schedule. A schedule gives your dog parameters. When he knows that he will go out at a certain time

A change in diet and feeding on a regular schedule may help prevent housetraining accidents.

(and all dogs have clocks in their heads), he will be more inclined to "hold it." If there is no schedule, he is liable to think, "Hmm. Gotta go. Might as well be now rather than later. Who knows when my human will think of it?" Scheduling applies to place as well as time. Take your dog to the same spot for his duties, and he will soon associate that spot with his elimination. It usually works best to select a spot in a direct visual line from the door so that the puppy can anticipate it.

10. **Contain your dog.** Restrict your dog's access to vulnerable rooms. If necessary, use a crate or confine him to a small tiled bathroom. Unhousetrained dogs have difficulty in perceiving the entire house as their "den," so incremental steps may work wonders.

11. **Get a dog door.** You can allow your dog access to the fenced-in yard via a doggy door when you are not home.

A dog door will allow your pet access to the yard when you're not home.

12. **Pay attention.** One mark of smarter-than-a-dog status is the ability to figure out signs of impending elimination. Sometimes your dog will do something obvious—like walk to the door. Puppies are more likely to exhibit subtler signs: sniffing around, licking their paws or lips, circling, looking "puzzled," or if you are lucky—whining.

13. **Ignore submissive urination.** This natural puppy behavior is usually outgrown, although it can also be seen in rescued dogs who have been punished or abused. You can help by doing nothing. Just walk away and clean up the mess unobtrusively later. If you scold your dog, he won't know why because he has done what he can to win your approval. Keep your dog's stress level low, and don't stare at or bend over him. If you have absolutely no other choice, your vet can prescribe phenylpropanolamine or other medications that improve urethral tone. These medications should be taken in addition to other training.

14. **Be patient with excitement urination.** Take it easy. Don't overexcite your dog by going overboard on the greetings yourself. The more relaxed and low-key you are, the less likely your dog is to go crazy. This behavior almost inevitably cures itself as your puppy matures and develops stronger sphincter control.

Never scold your dog for a housetraining accident; this will only increase his stress and make him more likely to repeat the behavior.

What Not to Do

Housetraining success depends on your constant supervision and kind attitude. Anything hinting of neglect or punishment will backfire.

1. **Just let your dog out.** While you may understand what your dog is supposed to accomplish, he may not. Dogs who are just turned outside with no guidance from their humans tend to simply hang around the back door and wait to be let in. Puppies in particular have short attention spans and forget why they are out there.

2. **Rub your dog's nose in his own excrement.** This practice is dirty, dangerous, cruel, and ineffective.

3. **Hit your dog.** Never hit your dog, even with a rolled-up newspaper. Pain and even fear of impending pain will just make your dog afraid of you.

4. **Yell or scold him.** Loud noises produce the same kind of painful visceral reactions that pain does: increase in blood pressure, slowing of intestinal motility, and other reactions stemming from the release of hormones like epinephrine and corticosteroids into the blood. This is really a bad idea for dogs exhibiting submissive urination. It will stress your dog and make it harder for to him to learn. You'll only increase his stress and make him more likely to repeat the behavior.

5. **Withhold water.** This can lead to bladder stones or even worse problems.
6. **Attempt to comfort a submissive dog.** He may regard it as a reward and repeat the behavior.
7. **Keep your dog crated for hours.** Dogs can "hold it" for only so long. Besides, crating a dog for long hours makes him depressed and anxious and can actually make housetraining (and other problems) worse. I would not keep any dog in a crate longer than two hours, except at night when he is supposed to be asleep. Even when traveling, take a potty break every couple of hours to let him stretch his limbs.
8. **Greet your dog with wild abandon.** That can trigger excitement urination. Always remain low-key and calm, and if your dog makes a mistake, ignore it for the time being (or at least don't make a huge fuss about cleaning it up).

TRAINING CHECKLIST

✓ Supervise your dog.
✓ Give him ample and scheduled opportunities to eliminate.
✓ Contain him when necessary.
✓ Go outside with your dog.
✓ Stay calm; never yell or hit him for making a mistake.

Chapter 14

Hyperactivity

Every day I hear people call their dogs "hyperactive." If pressed to define the term, owners may say "Well, he runs around all the time, never sits still, and is always into something. Honestly, he is DRIVING ME CRAZY!" However tempting it is to slap a medical diagnosis on such behavior, most of the time it's unwarranted.

ndeed, most behavior labeled "hyperactive" is not true medically diagnosed hyperactivity. It sounds paradoxical, but like all paradoxes, it is true. What most owners call hyperactivity is simply the result of a dog not getting enough exercise for his breed type, age, and natural activity level. Most "excessive" doggy activity is excessive for the owner, not the dog. Owner-labeled hyperactivity may be accompanied by a collection of similar unwanted behavior, including excessive vocalizing, housetraining difficulties, and destruction. (This is a tip-off that the dog may be experiencing an underlying condition, such as separation anxiety—see Chapter 19.)

True hyperactivity is a medical condition related to attention deficit disorder (ADD) in people. A truly hyperactive dog may have unfocused eyes; frantic, obsessive pacing; and other compulsive behaviors like tail spinning. His movements are nonstop.

Causes

True hyperactivity is generally medical in origin, but as in people, it's not well understood. For the average "overenergetic" dog, the causes are many and varied.

A truly hyperactive dog will display signs such as unfocused eyes and compulsive behaviors like tail spinning.

Medical Conditions

True hyperactivity (also called hyperkinesis) is rare in dogs.

While true medical hyperactivity can occur in any breed, very active breeds include the Dalmatian.

- **Neurological disorder.** Hyperkinesis is a rare abnormality associated with a neurological disorder, often involving imbalances in neurotransmitters. True hyperactivity must be diagnosed and treated by a veterinarian. Oddly enough, the condition is usually treated with amphetamines. No one is sure how it works, and most people fail to keep their dogs on the medication for the prescribed length of time. However, if they follow doctor's orders, the condition often resolves itself and further medication can be discontinued. In other cases, drugs like clomipramine can be used.
- **Medications.** Some medications, such as thyroid hormone supplements that overstimulate the thyroid, medications for female "leaking," and bronchodilators, can produce hyperactivity in some dogs.

Wolf Heritage

We don't know enough about wolf behavior to determine whether wolves suffer from hyperactivity or not. They certainly do not suffer the kind of environmentally induced lack of exercise that afflicts many modern dogs. However, wolves are extremely active animals by nature. Their home territory can cover hundreds of square miles (km), so it's hard to tell when a wild wolf is truly hyperactive. No one wants to get close enough to find out.

Breed Predilection and Genetics

While true medical hyperactivity can occur in any breed, very active breeds include the following:

- Chihuahuas
- Dalmatians
- English Springer Spaniels
- Foxhounds and coonhounds

High-Energy-Level Dogs

Interest in dogs with high energy levels is increasing. Today, about 50 percent of American Kennel Club- (AKC) registered breeds can be categorized as high energy. In 1915, only about 35 percent were so categorized. This is obviously a problem because a much larger percentage of the public is urban, an environment in which obtaining sufficient exercise for a dog is a challenge.

Dogs with lower levels of hyperactivity include the Basset Hound, Bloodhound, Bulldog, Newfoundland, and Saint Bernard. Note that the level of activity is not necessarily commensurate with size. Some large breeds need comparatively little exercise, while some tiny breeds like Chihuahuas need a lot—for their size. Understand, of course, that this doesn't mean that your Chihuahua needs to run a marathon. Toy dogs can get most of their exercise needs zooming around the house. However, you should still take them out for walks, for socialization in addition to exercise.

- Many herding breeds (Border Collies, Australian Shepherds)
- Most terrier breeds
- Nordic breeds, like Siberian Huskies Pomeranians
- Setters and pointing breeds

It's not always clear why some breed tends toward a higher level of activity. Some obviously need lots of energy to carry out their historical duties of herding or hunting. In Pomeranians, we can assume it's because they were "bred down" from larger, highly active spitz-type dogs, but with others we just don't know.

Environmental Factors

Many dogs are hyperkinetic for two simple reasons:

- **Lack of exercise.** Most dogs don't get enough exercise (and are also overweight). It is not enough for owners to have a large fenced-in yard. Most dogs will not self-exercise. They want you to play with them or take them for a run.
- **Boredom.** Dogs need to exercise their minds as well as their bodies. Give your dog something to think about. Even a few minutes of training, food puzzles, and flying disk can improve his outlook and calm him down.

What to Do

Think about the life your dog leads, especially when you are not home. Now is your chance to make it up to him and enrich his life. Your dog wants to be calm and well behaved. With your help, he can be.

1. **Provide lots of exercise time.** Join your dog in high-energy games! Even if you aren't a world-class sprinter or jogger, play fetch or flying disk with your high-energy dog. The key is regularity. When dogs expect exercise at regular intervals, they tend to be quieter at other times. On the other hand, if you exercise your dog only sporadically, he has no clue as to when to expect the next opportunity to release his energy and may become destructive.

2. **Provide mental stimulation.** Thinking uses energy and focuses attention. Taking your dog to training classes provides both of these, as well as crucial socialization. You can also teach your dog some tricks!

3. **Get into structured activities.** Many structured activities combine physical and mental stimulation. Here are just a few that can take the edge off a highly active dog: **Agility:** The sport of navigating various obstacles over a timed course. A sport for any breed or mix of any size. Topnotch agility dogs include Shetland Sheepdogs, Tervurens, Border Collies, Australian Shepherds, Golden Retrievers, Labrador Retrievers, Cocker Spaniels, Welsh Corgis, Parson/Jack Russell Terriers, and Papillons. **Bikejoring:** The sport of riding a mountain bike overland while being pulled by one or two dogs. Any fast, strong dog of medium or large size can participate. Sled dogs are naturals if the weather is sufficiently cool. **Canicross:** The sport of running cross-country with a dog attached and pulling you. This sport is for any of the sled-pulling breeds (when the weather is sufficiently cool). Other breeds that excel include tall hounds, pointers and setters, Dalmatians, Border Collies, and mixes. **Dock diving:** The sport of leaping from a stationary dock and retrieving objects thrown in the water. Top breeds include retrievers and water-loving mixes. Even small breeds like Jack/Parson Russell Terriers can do well at this event. **Flyball:** A team sport in which dogs race over hurdles, punch a spring-loaded box to grab a ball, and return. Any quick dog, large or small, can participate. **Flying disk:** A sport in which dogs and humans play Frisbee. Retrievers and herding breeds excel, but any breed or mix can compete. **Herding:** A sport in which dogs move sheep, cattle, or even ducks around in an assigned pattern. This organized sport is generally limited to herding breeds, although

THE EXPERT SAYS

According to dog breeder, trainer, and rescuer Sheila Boneham, Ph.D., "Often dogs are labeled 'hyperactive' when they are simply normal, healthy dogs who don't get enough exercise. Seeing that your dog gets the exercise he needs every day, as appropriate for his breed, age, and general health, should be your first step in managing abundant energy."

Don't expect your dog to self-exercise—daily structured playtime with you is the best way to ensure that he expends some energy.

herding mixes are equally capable. **Lure coursing:** A lure-chasing sport developed especially for sighthounds, but other dogs can compete in informal trials. I have a Dalmatian mix who excels at this. **Scootering:** A sport in which one or more harnessed dogs pull a scooter. Any strong, well-conditioned dog can participate. Alaskan Malamutes, German Shorthaired Pointers, Rottweilers, and Siberian Huskies excel. **Skijoring:** A sport in which a skier is pulled overland by one or more dogs. Strong, cold-weather breeds and mixes excel. **Sledding:** Sledding or mushing is a sport in which dogs pull a sled. Strong, cold-weather breeds and mixes excel. For information on these and more activities, see my book *The Encyclopedia of Dog Sports and Activities* (TFH Publications, Inc., 2009).

4. **Reward and reinforce quiet time.** Give food treats and verbal praise to your calm dog. However, remember that he must have sufficient exercise before you can reasonably expect him to calm down.

5. **Be calm yourself.** Dogs pick up clues from their owners; excitable people tend to have excitable dogs.

6. **Maintain control.** If this means using a head halter, do so. (Some are designed in such a way that they can be left on all the time.) You may also consider taking your dog to an obedience class, where he will learn to follow your commands.

7. **Provide plenty of interactive toys and food puzzles.** Rotate them at least once a week to ensure novelty and prevent boredom.

8. **Neuter your dog.** Unneutered dogs are much more active than their spayed counterparts. They also tend to vocalize more.

IF ALL ELSE FAILS

For true, veterinarian-diagnosed, neurologically based hyperactivity, try medication. Ironically enough, it was discovered that truly hyperactive dogs could be treated with methylphenidate, a stimulant, or a similar medication. Once again, this condition is very rare, so it is extremely unlikely that your dog suffers from it. Do not use diazepam or another sedative unless so directed by your veterinarian.

What Not to Do

Approach this problem with common sense and avoid unproductive "cures" like the following:

1. **Expect your dog to "self-exercise."** Some people think that just turning their dog loose in the backyard will solve the excess energy problem. However, most dogs are so dependent on humans for their well-being that even high-energy dogs will just stand around the yard looking bored until you come out and provide some structured high-energy playtime.

2. **Ignore it.** Ignoring a dog's need to exercise is not only cruel but may also rebound to your detriment. High-energy dogs need to exercise, and if you don't supply the opportunity, they will create their own: for example, digging, chewing, and ripping up furniture. The term "stir-crazy" comes to mind.

3. **Punish your dog.** Punishing an overexcited dog will only tend to make him fearful.

4. **Feed a low-protein diet.** Never feed your dog a low-protein diet in the hopes of controlling his behavior. It is a complete myth that dogs on low-protein diets will calm down. If they do, it's only because they are sick from the diet. (This myth got started when it was discovered that low-protein diets quell hyperactivity in rats. Rats are not dogs.)

TRAINING CHECKLIST

✓ Give your dog plenty of opportunities to exercise, preferably with you.
✓ Reward him with attention when he is quiet.
✓ Consider getting involved in dog-centered activities like agility or sledding.

Chapter 15

Inappropriate Sexual Behavior

"Inappropriate" is a kind of funny word. We use it to mean "not proper." In humans, inappropriate sexual behavior may include lewd comments, perusing pornography, or rape. Dogs, of course, don't do any of these things. They are completely natural animals. So, when we talk about canine sexually inappropriate behavior, we usually mean behavior that simply embarrasses or annoys us.

M any people find their pet's sexual behavior both disturbing and unnerving. This embarrassing behavior is all too common among the canine set, especially when it is directed at human beings rather than at other dogs.

Unspayed female dogs have a disconcerting tendency to go into heat twice a year, and intact males display all the annoying features of randy males in general. Males engage in sexual mounting behavior (vulgarly called "humping") even as puppies; it is part of their normal play behavior and practice for adulthood. As they mature, the mounting behavior becomes less associated with play, however, and is more directly addressed to female dogs in heat.

Male dogs engage in sexual mounting behavior even as puppies—it is part of their normal play behavior.

However, neutered males and even some female dogs may display mounting behavior, which although technically a sexual behavior, has other meanings. Some experts associate mounting with dominance display, although some new research indicates that it is merely a social overture that occurs during play. It is a normal behavior that occurs most often when the dog is in a state of emotional (not necessarily sexual) arousal. Mounting is most commonly seen in adolescent dogs, who like adolescent human beings, get all mixed up about sex and emotions.

Causes

Dogs have simpler psychologies than we do, so it may come as a bit of relief to know that however the problem started, it probably had little to do with an Oedipal complex.

Medical Conditions

- **Early bouts of sickness.** Research by Andrew Jagoe, internationally acclaimed dog authority (1994), indicates that dogs who experienced sickness as puppies are more likely than other dogs to exhibit abnormal sexual behavior later.
- **Compulsive disorder.** Mounting and masturbating can become a compulsive habit in dogs, which can then interfere with their normal functioning.
- **Urinary tract infections and skin allergies.** These can both lead to irritation that the dog is trying to scratch. I won't go into detail here, but you probably understand the problem.

Wolf Heritage

Wolves go into heat only once a year and so may be considered less highly sexed than their domestic counterparts. They are, for instance, monogamous, which dogs are not. The male canine desire to mate with anything at all at any time is a deviation from his noble ancestor's "high moral standards." In wolves, as a group, there is but one mating season. After that, all the wolves in the pack are exhausted and behave themselves. Not so with dogs.

Breed Predilection and Genetics

I have noticed that this behavior seems more common in smaller breeds, but that may not reflect its real incidence. There is, at any rate, no overriding prevalence of this behavior in any particular breed.

THE EXPERT SAYS

Dog trainer and rescue dog behavior consultant Sandy Getz says, "Mounting is not merely a sexual behavior but often a posturing behavior to show dominance or to test social ranking. Often with unaltered dogs, mounting behavior is seen in an attempt to mate. In most cases with altered dogs (male or female), it is merely a test to see whether he is the boss or not, perhaps even a sign of insecurity ('I am the boss, right??')."

Environmental Factors

Although sexual behavior is, of course, bred in the bone, so to speak, environmental factors can affect how it is displayed.

- **Affection.** Believe it or not, and unpleasant as it is, mounting behavior may simply be a way for a dog to show you how attached he is to you. Children especially, who are unaware of the significance of the behavior, are apt to encourage it.
- **Stress.** Some dogs respond to stress by mounting behavior.
- **Power grab.** Some dogs use mounting behavior as an attempt to climb higher on the doggy social ladder.

What to Do

Try to remember that this is a natural behavior, and don't get too upset about it. Most dog problems are more serious than this one.

1. **Neuter your dog.** Unless you are a breeder, there is no point in keeping an intact animal. Neutering a dog resolves this problem completely in about 25 percent of dogs and improves the behavior by 50 percent in another 70 percent of dogs.
2. **Walk away.** If your dog is practicing this annoying behavior on you, walk away. Try not to give the behavior any other attention.
3. **Offer a trade.** If your dog approaches you with that "look" in his eye, give him a toy or chew to distract him. It's the doggy equivalent of a cold shower.
4. **Interfere.** If your dog is mounting another dog who doesn't appreciate the attention, distract him with an alternate behavior, such as the *sit*. (See Chapter 4: Training Basics.) If your dog does not obey you, simply insert your body between the pair and tell the offender to cut it out. Firmly. Then give both dogs a cooling-off period.
5. **Reward less embarrassing behavior.** When your dog is behaving appropriately, shower him with affection.
6. **Teach the *leave it*.** This behavior will help your dog understand that a human leg is not his plaything. (See Chapter 4: Training Basics.)

When your dog is behaving appropriately, shower him with affection.

What Not to Do

It's easy to get all worked up over your dog's behavior, but don't let that spill over into making a serious mistake in correcting it.

1. **Let it continue.** Even if, for some unaccountable reason, this behavior does not annoy you, it can annoy your friends. Other dogs may also take unkindly to it, and a fight could develop.
2. **Punish your dog.** Your dog will do much better if prevented or distracted.

TRAINING CHECKLIST

✓ Neuter your dog.
✓ Walk away if the behavior is directed against you.
✓ Reward good behavior.
✓ Interfere immediately if your dog is bothering another dog or person.

Chapter 16

Jealousy

According to a study by the American Kennel Club (AKC), eight out of ten dog owners consider their dogs to be part of their family. Even more interestingly, a British survey found that 25 percent of dog owners would choose a pet over their mate if forced to make a choice. And who can blame them, really?

To prevent jealousy issues, it's usually best for the family dog not to sleep in his human's bed.

Dogs have no interest in politics, philosophy, or religion. They don't care about their owner's race, sexual orientation, criminal record, ethnic heritage, gender, weight, hairstyle, salary, age, housekeeping ability, or party affiliation. Any human being competent enough to get supper on the floor at a reasonable hour and who has a couch is good enough. If she hands out treats or belly rubs, so much the better.

While dogs may indeed be our best friends, the sad truth is that our close connections with them can lead to stress in our human relationships. Sometimes dogs become jealous of a new child, roommate, or spouse. And sometimes it's the human who becomes jealous of the dog, possibly with good reason. There are dog owners who feed their pets prime rib and serve their family beans. They spend hours walking and playing with their dogs and forget to pick up their child from soccer practice. I once knew a woman who insisted on owning several heavily shedding dogs despite the fact that her children were severely allergic to them.

One of the biggest points of contention occurs when partners argue about whether or not dogs should be allowed in bed. In almost all cases, this should be discouraged, not least because studies have shown that sleeping with dogs prevents humans from getting a good night's sleep. Even the smallest canine, it seems, can expand to almost unlimited size during the night and take up the entire bed to displace your partner.

Many times, the problem with the pet is just a cover-up for deeper underlying issues in a relationship. Especially in couples without children, the pets become a weapon against the partner in the same way that kids can become weapons in larger families.

Dogs can also be jealous of other dogs, of course. In such a case, they may become aggressive to the hated rival, or more subtly, attempt to draw the owner's attention away from the other dog to themselves, often by pawing and whining.

Causes

Jealousy is a complex emotion, and it's only recently that scientists have admitted that dogs are capable of feeling this emotion. Its causes are undoubtedly as complex as its manifestations.

Medical Conditions

Feelings of jealousy are natural and are not indicative that there is anything medically wrong with your dog, although it is just possible that he has a neurological condition that is making him act oddly.

Wolf Heritage

Not enough studies have been done on this topic to make a blanket statement, but it seems conceivable that wolves occasionally experience the green-eyed monster.

Breed Predilection and Genetics

A 2006 study by Paul Morris, of the University of Portsmouth, revealed that dogs feel all kinds of jealousy, including sexual jealousy and jealousy when a new person enters the family. While it seems logical to assume that guard breeds and one-person dogs (dogs attached primarily to one person rather than the whole family) are most prone to jealousy, and pack-oriented dogs less so, it's a highly individual thing that is difficult to measure.

THE EXPERT SAYS

Professional dog trainer Teoti Anderson, CPDT-KA, KPA-CTP, warns, "If your dog growls when your significant other approaches, he's not really being protective in the sense that he's afraid the other person will hurt you and he wants to keep you safe. He's actually protecting you as 'his'— it's called resource guarding. And you're the resource! If this occurs, or if you think that your dog may be 'jealous' of your new baby or is not getting along with a new roommate, don't try to solve the problem on your own. Please call a reward-based professional trainer to assist you before someone gets bitten."

Environmental Factors

The jealous dog is part of a competitive household, whether anyone else in the house realizes it or not. The chance of rivalry between dogs increases exponentially with every new human (or sometimes dog) added to the household. In many cases of dog–human jealousy, the object of envy is of the same sex as the dog. Whether this is just happenstance or deeper forces are at work is hard to say.

What to Do

When such a complex emotion is at work, be prepared to be flexible and creative.

1. **Take note(s).** Assess the level and kind of attention-seeking behavior your dog displays. Keep a log or journal for a week or two, noting times, places, and specific circumstances associated with the behavior. If you must take your dog to a trainer or veterinarian, she will need this information. Video-record the behavior if possible.
2. **Use counterconditioning.** One good way to satisfy everyone is to take a long walk, just the three of you. It works when adding another dog to the family, and it will work now. The dog will associate your new person with pleasant things. Long walks (even if not on the beach) are

romantic, and at the end of it, you'll know enough about your date to decide whether to let her (or him) back in the house for a nightcap or to say, "Whew, I'm just exhausted after all that. It's been fun. Good night."

3. **Use affection control.** Lowering the attention given to your dog is the single most effective action you can take. In other words, giving him the cold shoulder is the best tactic— tough love at its finest. If you are constantly fussing with your dog when it's just you and him and then ignore him when your significant other stops by, don't be surprised when your dog resents it. Your choices are to lower your dog's affection expectation in general or else continue to carry on with your dog like a lovesick dodo even when you have a viable date in the room with you. When you do decide to interact with your dog, it must indeed be your decision. Never allow a jealous dog to initiate contact.

4. **Have the new person begin to interact with the dog in a positive way.** The hated rival should start feeding your dog meals, giving him treats, and taking him for walks (just the two of them). Soon the dog will associate only good things with the newbie.

5. **Reassign your dog's sleeping quarters.** Since one hopes this isn't a sudden decision on your part, try retraining your dog to accept a different place when you and your beloved are alone together. Do not try this just when your date is there, or your dog will naturally associate his perceived loss of status with the new rival. You could

> Lowering the attention given to your jealous dog is the single most effective action you can take.

If your dog is jealous of another dog, try taking them on walks together and award special treats only when both dogs are present.

invest in a new larger couch or even a bigger bed, but it's wiser to simply establish a different place for your dog to sleep. Use high-value treats, praise, and exercise to make your point. Try giving him a Nylabone or other long-lasting interactive toy. Remember to work on this when you are alone with your dog. With proper motivation, this should only take a couple of days.

6. **Make dog–dog interactions positive.** If your dog is jealous of another dog, try to make his experience with his rival as pleasant as possible. Take them on walks together, and award special treats only when both dogs are present. The main idea is to get your dog to associate only pleasant things with his rival.

7. **Be patient.** If you want to go forward with your human relationship, be patient. Both people and dogs need time to warm up to each other. It's important to make both feel important. For dogs, routine is critical, so as much as possible, don't mess with things like his feeding routine.

What Not to Do

It's important to remember that your dog is a dog. Treating him too much like a person can make things worse. Don't do any of the following:

IF ALL ELSE FAILS

Sometimes it really does come down to choosing between your pet and your partner (or other pets). This is a decision that only you can make. I acquired my most recent dog from just such a situation.

1. **Spoil the dog.** Spoiling a dog unfairly raises his expectations. This may sound strange, but according to James Serpell, Professor of Animal Welfare and Director of the Center for the Interaction of Animals and Society at the University of Pennsylvania, much of the trouble arises from allowing your dog to get too close to you. Letting your dog sleep in the same bed with you not only disturbs a night's sleep but gives the animal an elevated notion of his own importance. Your bed becomes his territory, which he will defend against strangers.

2. **Ignore the problem.** In some cases, jealousy can lead to aggression.

TRAINING CHECKLIST

✓ Lower your dog's expectations.
✓ Give your dog appropriate affection.
✓ Keep your dog out of your bed.

Chapter 17

Jumping Up

Jumping up is classic attention-seeking behavior. The dog is usually focused on your face, which he wants to sniff; his tail is wagging and his expression is happy. And "happy" is the key word here. The reason most dogs jump is because they are happy to see you. You may have inadvertently encouraged this behavior in the past; it's often "cute" to see a puppy jump. However, the cuteness fades as the puppy slowly turns into a giant Newfoundland. Luckily, there is a pretty quick fix to the problem.

Your first goal is to stop rewarding the jumping. "What reward?" you might grumble. "It's not like I hand out a dog biscuit or something every time he knocks me down." Assuredly not, but remember, a dog's world is not your world. Human attention and contact may be all that your dog is looking for. This is behavior that you can pretty well predict, so get ready for it.

Causes

To discover the causes for leaping up, we need look no farther than anatomy, physiology, and canine culture.

Medical Conditions

There are really no medical conditions that cause a dog to jump up except for possibly the following:

- **Hyperactivity.** In this condition, an overproduction of adrenalin translates into jumping, as well as other over-the-top energy expenditures. (See Chapter 14: Hyperactivity.)

Wolf Heritage

Fortunately, wolves are not in the habit of jumping up on people.

- **Food retrieval.** However, wolf pups will jump up and pull at their parents' jowls in an attempt to get food, which is subsequently regurgitated to them. So dogs have inherited the same tendency, although, of course, today breeders feed their young puppies mush starting at an early age.

Breed Predilection and Genetics

Dogs of any breed, including toy breeds, can engage in this behavior. It is, however, most common in young dogs, mostly because of their excessive energy level and efforts to get near your face (for food, presumably).

- **Greeting behavior.** This is again a function of wolf behavior, going back to puppyhood, when puppies greeted their mothers in an attempt to get dinner.
- **Excitement and arousal.** Dogs and humans jump up and down from excitement. All that adrenalin flowing through us makes us want to go somewhere, and if we can't (or don't want to) run, we jump and leap in the air for sheer excitement.

Environmental Factors

Jumping occurs in two primary situations:

- **Greeting.** Your dog is delighted to see you and wants to get as close to your face as possible, as required in dog culture. The only way to do this is to jump.
- **Play.** Playing around includes jumping around, and jumping, in people as well as dogs, is a natural behavior. Sometimes, though, it can be a rough experience, at least with larger dogs.

What to Do

This behavior is relatively easy to redirect.

1. **Give the cold shoulder.** If your dog jumps up, respond by folding your arms and turning your body away. Walk away. Say nothing. Don't even look at him. In a few minutes, when he is calmer, you can quietly praise him. He will soon learn that the positive attention he seeks will be gained when he is quiet and relaxed.

2. **Refocus his attention.** Keep some chew treats or toys in your pocket. As soon as you walk in the door, throw the treat away from you on the floor. Most dogs will immediately turn away from you and go for the treat. Reward him with quiet attention only when he has all four feet on the floor.

3. **Offer behavioral options.** Another way to approach the problem is by offering him an alternate behavior. Giving your dog a way to greet guests other than knocking them unconscious will make everyone happier. When he charges toward you or your friends, tell him "Sit" (not angrily). The instant he obeys, give him a treat and the attention he longs for. Even the smartest dog in the world can't jump and sit at the same time. (Instead of sitting, you might ask your dog to lie down or "go to bed," but the principle is the same. The *sit*, however, is the most useful command because it can be used to curb an overexuberant pet on a walk. [See Chapter 4: Training Basics.])

4. **Practice good greetings.** Give your dog lots of practice at this behavior, preferably with a willing collaborator. This is an especially important behavior to teach when the dog is jumping up on

Dogs often jump up when greeting their humans and during playtime.

If your dog jumps up when greeting you at the door, throw a treat on the floor to refocus his attention on something else.

THE EXPERT SAYS

Dog breeder, trainer, and rescuer Sheila Boneham, Ph.D., says, "It's easier to teach your dog to do something than to not do something, so to teach him not to jump up, give him an alternative behavior such as *sit* or *down*. He jumps up to get attention, so anticipate when he's likely to jump up and give the alternate command before he does. Then reward him. He'll learn that he doesn't get the attention he wants by jumping on people, but he does get attention when he sits and waits politely."

visitors. While you might be able to stalk off in a dignified way, your great Aunt Hattie may not be able to. If your dog can stay quietly for ten seconds with all four on the floor, praise him.

5. **Get down to his level.** This technique should be used mostly for young puppies. As he comes toward you, crouch down for a face-to-face greeting, but slide your thumb under his collar at the chin to encourage him to keep all four on the floor. As he does, praise him gently. You don't want him to get any more excited than he already is.

What Not to Do

While following the above directions will probably succeed, doing any of the following will set your efforts way, way back.

1. **Reward the behavior by yelling "No!"** For dogs, even negative attention is behavioral reinforcement. Avoid the temptation.

2. **Shove him in the chest.** This could hurt your dog and will do nothing to stop the behavior. He may think that you're playing. Larger, more athletic dogs

will take this as a playful challenge and will push back.

3. **Step on his toes.** Don't step on his toes, either. You could seriously injure your dog.
4. **Pet your dog on the hind legs.** This will encourage him to jump up, possibly by stimulating the nerves in the legs, although no one is really sure why this occurs.

Chapter 18

Self-Mutilation and Other Obsessive-Compulsive Behaviors

Obsessive-compulsive disorder (OCD) is characterized by time-consuming, repetitive behaviors, such as constant licking, nail biting, fly snapping, and chewing. It is similar to compulsive hand washing or hair pulling in human beings. This is truly abnormal behavior, unlike barking or digging, for it serves no natural purpose and is not beneficial to the animal (except possibly to help relieve his stress). Many, if not most, of these behaviors have begun as either medical problems or attention-seeking behaviors. However, scientists are more and more recognizing that a strong genetic component is at work as well.

Causes

Self-mutilation has been observed in most animal species, including our own. It has various causes.

Medical Conditions

Some kinds of obsessive-compulsive behaviors, such as nail biting and chewing, may originate from any of the following conditions:

- **Skin infection.** Any bacterial, viral, or fungal condition can irritate the skin and start a dog on the path to self-mutilation. In his attempt to soothe the itch, he only exacerbates the problem, just like humans do with a bad case of poison ivy.
- **Demodectic mange.** Demodectic mange is an infection caused by a mite. It makes dogs intensely itchy and desperate to scratch and chew at the affected spot.
- **Wound or injury.** There might be a thorn, sharp stone, or other foreign object in the pads between the toes, causing your dog to worry at the spot.
- **Hormonal imbalance.** Your dog may be producing too little thyroid hormone or too much cortisol. Both of these can lead to skin infections and the urge to lick.
- **Dry skin.** He may also simply have dry skin, caused by dry weather or not enough fatty acids in the diet. Dry skin is itchy skin.
- **Allergies.** Common allergies include mold and pollen, pesticides, and soaps. In some cases, a food allergy could be to blame.

Obsessive-compulsive disorder (OCD) is characterized by time-consuming, repetitive behaviors, such as constant licking.

If your dog is constantly scratching, check him for fleas.

- **Nerve damage.** Sometimes there may be or have been irritation to the nerves that supply part of the tail, which can induce "tail checking" or tail chasing.
- **Fleas.** If your dog has fleas, they will be most numerous on the abdomen, base of the tail, and on the head. But they could be anywhere. Other than seeing real live fleas, signs include their dark, gritty "flea dirt" (otherwise known as flea excrement), hair loss, scabs, and of course, furious scratching on the part of the dog. Some dogs are so sensitive to fleabites that it only takes one little nip to set off a terrible itch–scratch cycle, which may eventually lead to compulsive licking.
- **Retinal artery remnants.** Retinal artery remnants in the aqueous humor of the eye can cause a behavior called "fly snapping." This means that the dog is "seeing" something that is in his eye, not in the environment—it looks like flies to him, which he obsessively snaps at. The eye "floaters" that some people have is a similar phenomenon.
- **Medicines.** Some medications, including non-steroidal anti-inflammatory drugs (NSAIDs) and antibiotics, may cause nausea, which lead to obsessive licking in a dog's attempt to soothe himself.
- **Dental disease.** This can cause oral pain that leads to licking in an attempt to relieve pain.
- **Canine cognitive dysfunction (CCD).** This is a disease of aged dogs, similar to Alzheimer's disease in humans, that compels them to act in all sorts of odd ways they never did before.

Wolf Heritage

Wolf heritage may also be responsible for some obsessive-compulsive behaviors. In addition, licking, which is the start of the problem, is a very natural behavior in both dogs and wolves.

- **Flea destruction.** In the wild, chewing and biting is the way to destroy fleas, so in that sense this is normal behavior in dogs today.

- **Shorten dewclaws.** Wolves bite their dewclaws nail to shorten them, but persistent chewing on them is not a normal behavior.

Breed Predilection and Genetics

Some breeds are definitely more prone to self-mutilation and OCD behaviors than others; specific heritable factors are involved.

- **CDH2 gene.** Scientists have now identified the actual gene responsible for compulsive behavior or that has at least conferred a high risk of compulsive disorder susceptibility. The work was done in a 2010 collaboration among the Behavior Service at the Cummings School of Veterinary Medicine, the Program in Medical Genetics at the University of Massachusetts Medical School, and the Broad Institute at the Massachusetts Institute of Technology.

  The troublesome gene is CDH2, which encodes cadherin-2, a protein involved in forming connections between neural cells. The CDH2 gene is expressed in the hippocampus, a region of the brain long suspected to be involved in these kinds of behaviors in people and animals. Although the link is not perfect, it was found that 60 percent of the dogs who obsessively chomped down and chewed their flanks, blankets, and anything else within teeth reach had the variant, compared with 43 percent of those with a milder chewing compulsion and only 22 percent of those with no signs of compulsive behavior. This is the first genetic locus identified for any animal compulsive disorder. It also raises the intriguing possibility that CDH2 and other neuronal adhesion proteins are involved in human autism spectrum disorder.

- **Natural grooming behavior.** Of course, some degree of licking is normal in dogs—it is a part of their natural grooming behavior. The most commonly afflicted breeds for obsessive licking, leading to lick granulomas, are:

- **Doberman Pinschers.** Dobermans are likely to exhibiting flank chewing and blanket sucking, a behavior linked to obsessive hand washing in people.
- **Bull Terriers.** A high proportion of Bull Terriers chase their tails relentlessly.
- **Great Danes.** Great Danes exhibit most forms of OCD behavior but most commonly acral lick dermatitis.
- **Labrador Retrievers.** Labs exhibit almost all forms and can become intensely focused on objects like balls and sticks (even beyond what is normal for a Labrador).
- **Border Collies.** Possibly as a result of their herding instinct, these dogs may often be neurotically anxious to round up vacuum cleaners, lawnmowers, and the like. They may also stare, hypnotized by reflective surfaces, and go crazy after imaginary flies.
- **Certain birddog breeds.** They exhibit fly-snapping behavior, as well as acral lick dermatitis.

Environmental Factors

It appears that certain problems in the environment can "turn on" a culprit gene or even initiate the behavior in dogs without the genetic component.

• **Boredom.** In a few cases, boredom has been pegged as the culprit, but this is far less common than used to be believed, as scientists learn more about the genetic factors involved. Still, boredom

Great Danes exhibit most forms of OCD behavior.

Labrador Retrievers exhibit almost all forms of OCD and can become intensely focused on objects like balls and sticks.

can play a part. As highly intelligent predators, dogs need activities. They are no longer free to run wild in the woods and streets and exercise their problem-solving abilities. Left to their own lonely devices in a confined space, they may start chewing—on themselves. You may have taught them not to chew on the sofa, but the urge to chew has not been destroyed altogether.

- **Stress.** Stressed dogs have few ways of taking out their frustrations. The behavior of the other house dogs, neglect, cramped quarters, screaming children, and similar things can raise the stress level in a dog until he starts chewing on himself (rather than on others, a solution that might also suggest itself from time to time).

What to Do

Once it becomes established, self-mutilation is an extremely difficult problem to cure. It almost always requires professional intervention. One easy rule: If the problem is caused by allergies, it will probably respond to corticosteroids. True OCDs will not. Unfortunately, that includes OCDs that started as allergic responses.

1. **Take note(s).** Assess the level and kind of the behavior. Videotaping is helpful as well. Keep a log for a week or two, noting times, places, and specific circumstances associated with the behavior. If you need to take your dog to a trainer or veterinarian, she will require this

information. Video-record the behavior if possible. Sadly, most owners do not report obsessive behaviors until they have become an established pattern, as at first glance they seem harmless and nondestructive. Or the owner may have attempted to comfort the dog displaying the behavior or present an attractive alternative. Sometimes this actually has the effect of reinforcing the compulsive behavior. If you determine that the behavior is related to excessive confinement, conflict, or boredom, these situations should be remedied as soon as possible.

2. **Determine the cause.** See a vet. If your dog has an allergy or infection, it must be treated right away. You can try an anti-itch spray to help heal and soothe the skin. Use one with a taste deterrent to help stop the behavior.

For cases of acral lick dermatitis, try a foot or leg bandage, which will disrupt the licking cycle and allow the limb to heal.

Changing your dog's environment, such as taking him for a car ride, can help with OCD behaviors.

3. **Change his environment.** It is sometimes effective to take the dog out of the environment where the behavior has been occurring. Outdoor exercise, rides in cars, or even a day at work with you may help.

4. **Medicate your dog.** Your vet may prescribe behavior-modifying medications. Some of these may require four to six weeks to take full therapeutic effect, so be patient. Commonly prescribed medications include selective serotonin reuptake inhibitors (SSRIs), like clomipramine and fluoxetine. In some cases, melatonin, an over-the-counter, natural hormone used to treat insomnia in people, works well on flank lickers. Special medications are also available for dogs with canine cognitive disorder.

5. **Keep him on a year-round flea preventive.** This applies to cases where the initiating cause was a fleabite. If necessary, treat your house and yard for these little buggers as well.

6. **Add fatty acids to the diet.** For cases of lick dermatitis, adding fatty acids to the diet may help. This works in the early stages if the problem is initiated by dry or irritated skin. After it becomes an established pattern, though, diet won't matter.

7. **Change the feeding schedule.** For a dog with obsessive licking, try giving smaller, more frequent meals with added fiber. These techniques tend to make a dog feel fuller, and it seems that dogs engage in obsessive licking most frequently when they are hungry.

8. **Try a leg or foot bandage.** For acral lick dermatitis, try a leg or foot bandage. This kind of bandage works much better than an Elizabethan collar, which, although effective in stopping the foot licking, may increase the stress on your dog to the point where other objectionable behaviors ensue. In addition, you may want to put a bitter-tasting agent on top of the bandage. This will help disrupt the licking cycle and may stop it altogether. I have used a white athletic sock, wrapped up

IF ALL ELSE FAILS

Try using an ultrasonic collar to distract the dog. There is no electric shock, just an ultrasonic noise or vibration (depending on the type).

in a self-sticking vet wrap bandage, with success.

9. **Prevent or discourage the behavior.** Encourage your dog to use tough, interactive chew toys, but be careful about presenting them as an immediate alternative; he might confuse the offered distraction as a reward for the compulsive behavior.

10. **Reduce boredom.** Try food puzzles, and give your dog as much freedom as possible for his safety. A dog who has to stay in a small room staring at four blank walls can go wacky in more ways than one.

11. **Add structure.** Dogs who have something definite to look forward to seem to be less likely to develop obsessive-compulsive behaviors. Walks, interactive play, and car rides can have astonishing effects.

What Not to Do

Remember that this problem is hard to eradicate, so be very patient. The following tactics are unproductive.

1. **Yell at your dog.** This simply increases the stress on the dog and adds impetus to an already serious situation.

2. **Reward your dog.** Never reward your dog by offering him an attractive distraction in the middle of the behavior. He may interpret this as praise for his actions.

TRAINING CHECKLIST

✓ Determine the cause of the behavior.
✓ Distract attention from or bandage the spot.
✓ Consider medical therapy.

Chapter 19

Separation Anxiety

Like humans, dogs are social creatures, and when they are separated from their family or pack, it is natural for them to feel some distress. When taken from their mother and littermates and placed within a home, nearly all puppies experience this uncomfortable and scary feeling. They may cry or whine during the night. In most cases, the anxiety disappears after a day or so, as the puppy quickly habituates to his new family.

Because dogs are bred to be our companions and partners, it is not surprising that leaving them alone triggers fearful and stressed behavior.

However, separation anxiety can also grow into a serious problem. Dogs with severe separation anxiety may bark incessantly, soil the rug, try to escape the home, or chew furniture and woodwork. Sadly, separation anxiety is the second-most-common reason (after aggression) why dogs are euthanized.

Causes

Complex behaviors like separation anxiety have a multitude of possible causes, ranging from the physical to the psychological.

Medical Conditions

A number of medical conditions can result in separation anxiety.

- **Early sickness.** Research by renowned canine researcher Andrew Jagoe in 1994 indicates that dogs who experienced sickness as puppies were most likely to have separation anxiety as adults. They were especially likely to vocalize excessively.
- **Canine cognitive dysfunction (CCD).** In older dogs, CCD, a neurological condition similar to Alzheimer's disease in humans, can cause separation anxiety.

Wolf Heritage

A dog's heritage can explain one cause of separation anxiety.

- **Wolves as pack animals.** Wolves are not used to being alone; they are pack animals, like dogs are. However, wolf puppies may be left alone for a considerable period of time by their parents while the latter are out hunting.

Breed Predilection and Genetics

We have selected dogs to become more dependent on us than wolf puppies are on their parents, and many dogs simply can't bear to be alone. Because dogs are bred to be our companions and partners, it is not surprising that leaving them alone triggers fearful and stressed behavior. They were never meant to be alone, and they plain don't like it. This is especially true for companionable breeds. Separation anxiety can and does occur in any breed with great frequency, but the following are often identified as being especially vulnerable:

- Weimaraners
- German Shepherd Dogs
- Airedale Terriers (many other kinds of terriers are not anxiety prone at all—interestingly, it is the Airedale who has a long history of working closely with human beings as war dogs and police dogs, unlike many other terriers, who lived in the barn and were kept mainly as rat killers)
- Mixed breeds (some reports suggest that mixed breeds are more prone to separation anxiety than purebreds, but my guess is that mixed breeds are more likely to be found in shelters—a primary trigger of later separation anxiety)

Having said all this, I want to emphasize that basic temperament is more important than breed type. And temperament is genetically influenced, although no specific genes are associated with separation anxiety.

SMART STUFF

The Second-Most-Common Disorder

Separation anxiety is the second-most-common problem in domestic dogs, after aggression. It is estimated that 16 percent of all dogs suffer from it, and that percentage is higher in dogs who come from shelters. Technically, separation anxiety is a psychological condition rather than a behavior. However, it results in a specific collection of behaviors, such as house soiling, barking, and destruction, which can be addressed together. If your dog is exhibiting these behaviors but is not suffering from separation anxiety, please see those specific chapters.

Environmental Factors

Because the home/family is the setting for separation anxiety, it is not surprising that it's also the main cause.

- **Sudden enforced separation.** The most common cause of separation anxiety in dogs seems to be a sudden period of enforced separation, which has been preceded by a relatively long period of close, warm contact. Such dogs seem to have become overdependent on their human caregiver. Rescued dogs, who have already been abandoned once, are much more likely to attempt to form strong bonds with their new owner and thus suffer incredible anxiety when the adopter inevitably leaves for work or school.

- **Lack of exercise.** Dogs who receive insufficient exercise are more likely to develop separation anxiety. Well-exercised dogs are filled with pleasant endorphins that make them calmer and happier. Besides, they are too tired to be stressed.

- **Prior abuse and neglect.** Abusive treatment destroys a dog's confidence and his ability to take charge of his time. I have noticed in my own dogs that those I have owned from puppyhood are self-confident and fearless when alone, but rescued dogs are famously plagued with anxiety of all sorts.

Because the home/family is the setting for separation anxiety, it is not surprising that it's also the main cause.

What to Do

It may take some time and the use of more than one kind of treatment, but separation anxiety can usually be cured or at least managed.

1. **Take note(s) or video-record what happens when you are gone.** Assess the level and kind of behavior. Keep a log for a week or two, noting times, places, and specific circumstances or triggers associated with the behavior. If you must take your dog to a trainer or veterinarian, she will need this information. Video-record the behavior if possible.

2. **Let a new puppy sleep in his own bed right next to you.** This eases fears and builds bonding between owner and dog. However, it is not always wise to allow the dog to actually share your bed. Studies show that people who sleep with their dogs have more problems in getting a good night's rest—dogs have the mysterious ability to swell up to four or five times their normal size

during the night and take over the entire bed. In addition, allowing a dog to share your bed may give him an inflated idea about his importance in the household, and that can spell trouble down the road. Dogs need their own beds, just like kids do.

3. **Exercise your dog.** A good hard run or other vigorous exercise prior to your departure will increase the dog's sense of well-being (providing those crucial endorphins). It will also wear him out. It's even better if you can get someone else to exercise him while you get ready to leave.

4. **Lower your dog's expectations.** A number of tactics can be used. Stop petting, kissing, and fooling around with your dog every minute you are around. One of the best ways is to train him that he can't have affection on demand. This is especially important during your arrival and departures. Your attitude should be cool and off-putting. Emotionally ignore your dog for 20 minutes before you leave and after you return. This will eventually remove the powerful emotional triggers associated with those events. It's tough, but you'll both be happier in the long run.

Dogs who receive insufficient exercise are more likely to develop separation anxiety.

5. **Practice distance or independence training.** Teach your dog to lie down on his own mat at a distance that is comfortable for him. Give him a special, long-lasting food treat (perhaps a food puzzle) that he would receive at no other time. This will reward your dog for displaying independence. Gradually increase the distance. He needs to learn that the world won't come to an end if his owner isn't in eyesight. Some experts recommend that during the training period you should keep your dog away from you behind a closed door 20 to 30 percent of the time.

6. **Disrupt the routine.** Don't get ready to leave the same way in the same order every day. As your dog sees the inevitable and progressive order of your impending departure, his tensions build up and he is predisposing himself to become anxious. By reordering your routine, he'll be off guard and less anxious.

THE EXPERT SAYS

Peggy Swager, well-known trainer, behaviorist consultant, and author of *Training the Hard to Train Dog*, says, "The key to solving separation anxiety is to improve your dog's self-confidence. One way to do this is to teach him to trust you as a strong and confident leader. Dogs pattern their behavior after yours. When you are strong and confident, they will be the same."

Many people have found that a swaddling-type vest decreases separation anxiety in their dogs.

7. **Wrap him up.** Just as some cultures swaddle babies to add to their feelings of security, many people have had great luck with a swaddling-type dog vest. A friend of mine put a vest like this on her new rescued dog and within minutes, instead of whining and pawing at her in desperation, he curled up on the futon and fell asleep. Until that point, the only thing that had worked was medication.

8. **Provide comfort items.** A voice recording of you or a worn, smelly old t-shirt or other piece of clothing may serve as an emotional prop while you are gone.

9. **Countercondition your dog.** Pair your departures with interactive food-stuffed treats that you give only when you are leaving. Don't make a huge emotional fuss about it, though—just drop the treat and leave.

10. **Systematically desensitize him.** Use this technique along with counterconditioning. Practice leaving your dog alone for very short periods (under a minute) and gradually increase the separation time. Keep a log recording how often you practice, how long you are gone, and your dog's reaction. For the fastest cure, practice several times a day.

You will also need to include departure cues as part of this process. Dogs are so clever at noting departure cues that their anxiety begins to build long before you leave the house. Most of us do the same things in the same order every day. (Weekends, of course, are different, and most dogs quickly learn to adjust their behavior to a weekend clock too.) Your dog may know that when you shove your cell phone in your purse or even start shaving that departure is imminent. Help your dog de-stress about

One way to ensure that your dog has something to do while you're not home is to hire a dog walker to take him out during the day.

these cues. On an off day, pick up the keys and walk around, but don't leave. Do similar things with your cell phone, briefcase, or whatever object is triggering the stress. As your dog becomes used to this and then brief departures, you can gradually increase the time away. The problem, of course, is that most of us live in the real world and have to be gone several hours a day even though we haven't finished desensitizing our dogs. And inserting that several-hour absence into the middle of the desensitizing procedure makes it almost worthless unless you can get a friend to babysit or leave your dog at a day care he enjoys. But wait—there's help on the way. It's called medication.

11. **Medicate your dog.** Anti-anxiety medications are extremely helpful in combating separation anxiety when used in conjunction with training. Dr. Katherine A. Houpt, James Law Professor of Behavior Medicine at Cornell University, notes that veterinarians can prescribe medications to treat separation anxiety. They serve to reduce the intensity that dogs feel when their owners leave. "These should NOT be used as a last resort," she counsels, "because these dogs are really suffering." However, these medications do not take full therapeutic effect for four to six weeks, although you may note a positive change after two or three weeks.

Because of the long "lead-in" time for many dogs, your vet may want to add diazepam or another short-acting anxiolytic with the other medication while it is building its therapeutic effect.

Dog-appeasing pheromones (DAP), once very trendy, may not be as effective in dealing with separation anxiety as was once thought.

As in cases of aggression, however, we don't know how well these drugs work over time, even if initial results are encouraging. There may also be changes in the neurotransmitter receptors in the brain that make the medication less beneficial in the long run. The beauty of medications, however, is that they facilitate training, making it easier for a dog to learn. Clomipramine works so well for some dogs that owners make the mistake of simply leaving their dog on medication without doing the requisite training. This is expensive and unnecessary. Proper training and behavior therapy will help your dog naturally attain and keep his mental equilibrium.

What Not to Do

Doing the wrong thing, even with the best intentions, will not only not cure the problem—it might make it worse.

1. **Crate the dog.** For humans, the simplest solution to separation anxiety—especially when it's destructive—seems to be the crate. Of course, a crated dog won't eat the furniture or poop on the floors. But he will still vocalize. A crate is no comfort to many dogs with separation anxiety; in fact, many will damage their teeth or paws trying to get out. Separation anxiety rapidly turns into barrier anxiety. If you have to contain your dog, try to provide as large a space as possible to decrease his anxiety, vocalizing, and destructive behavior.

Don't crate a dog with separation anxiety; he will become more stressed and could harm himself trying to get out.

IF ALL ELSE FAILS

...Or even if it doesn't! Hire a dog walker or consider day care. There is a statistically significant connection between the time a dog is left alone and the chances that he will engage in destructive behavior. Interestingly, there is no such link between barking and time left alone. In other words, a dog with separation anxiety may begin barking the instant the door closes but may not start eating the furniture until a considerable period of time has elapsed.

2. **Rely only on drugs.** Medications to treat separation anxiety should be an adjunct to training, not a replacement for it.

3. **React.** Even if you come home to a torn-up house, chewed furniture, and a guilty-looking dog, do not respond by yelling at him. But don't try to comfort him either. Silently repair the damage. Any response you make to the mess will trigger a response in your already overreactive dog, and it won't be a good one. Anything you do will be regarded by him as a reward for his behavior (bad idea) or a threat (worse idea).

TRAINING CHECKLIST

✓ Practice independence training and desensitizing methods.
✓ Give him appropriate attention (not too much and not too little).
✓ Consider medications as an adjunct to therapy.

Chapter 20

Shyness, Phobias, and Fears

For behaviorists, fears and phobias are not the same thing. A fear is considered to be a normal, natural reaction to a threatening situation. It serves a useful purpose—to protect the dog from harm. A phobia is much more intense; it is described as a persistent and irrational fear (out of proportion to the stimulus) and therefore can be considered a medical condition in itself. Many phobias are linked to specific items or objects: A dog may be healthy, happy, and outgoing until you get the vacuum cleaner out or the barometric pressure drops, indicating an impending thunderstorm.

Fearfulness is actually a desirable, protective, and adaptive trait, especially for wild and feral canids. It keeps them away from grizzly bears, rattlesnakes, and other natural dangers. Modern dogs, the product of thousands of years of domestication, are less fearful of new situations. However, even they are not completely free of due caution. An experiment performed years ago put cardiac monitors on dogs and found that when dogs ventured into new territory, their heart rates soared, indicating a high level of stress. A shy dog may move slowly and fearfully, in mincing steps, with his legs pulled under and neck extended—the better to look out for the enemy he imagines lurks everywhere. (This behavior can be seen in young captive wolves when they enter a large penned area for the first time.) Some dogs are generally shy and fearful; they are reluctant to meet strangers, dislike noise, and don't interact well with other dogs.

Phobias are common in dogs; in fact, it has been estimated that one-third of problem behaviors in dogs are directly related to fears. There is nothing at all abnormal about fear of thunder, for example. In the natural state, the only really loud noise is thunder, and thunder is the brother of lightning. Lightning really is dangerous. It kills dogs out in the open, and the smart thing to do when lightning is around is to take cover—which is exactly what your dog is doing.

Causes

Dogs can become shy for some of the same basic reasons we do: natural proclivity and environmental stress.

Fears and phobias are quite common in dogs, with an estimated one-third of problem behaviors related to these issues.

SMART STUFF

How Hearing Affects Phobias

Because a dog's hearing is more acute than a human's, extending into the ultrasound and infrasound ranges, an apparently unmotivated fear may have its source in something you yourself can't hear. Or a dog who may appear to be afraid of a certain location may actually be experiencing fear of a sound (or sight) he once experienced there.

With thunderphobia, for instance, one little rumble or a drop in barometric pressure sends some dogs to the cellar and others behind the toilet in a whining, quivering mass. Dogs with phobias shake, pace, cry, stare, salivate, shiver, whine, and huddle with their owners in the presence of the noisome (and usually noisy) stimulus. Some dogs become so terrified that they tear out a screen door or jump through a window in an effort to avoid the hated stimulus.

Medical Conditions

Experts have found that when a dog shows sudden shyness, disease is a likely culprit.

- **Early sickness.** Research by internationally known canine scientist Andrew Jagoe in 1994 has indicated that dogs who experienced a good deal of sickness as puppies were more likely than healthy puppies to develop fear of children and strangers.
- **Physical discomfort.** Pain (or fear of pain) of any kind can lead a dog to try to avoid human contact. Common culprits are hip dysplasia or neck or spine pain.
- **Hearing or visual impairment.** Many deaf or visually impaired dogs are also very shy as they have fewer ways to evaluate their environment and their safety.
- **Thyroid problems.** Dogs with low thyroid levels tend to have many accompanying behavioral quirks. Shyness can be one of them.
- **Ear infections.** Dog with sore ears will make serious attempts to keep their heads away from people.

Wolf Heritage

In the wolf world, shyness can pay off, especially if you're not strong enough to win a fight. He who runs away does indeed live to fight another day (maybe).

- **Hearing problems.** Thunderphobia is pretty common among dogs. While it's usually considered just another variety of noise phobia, thunder may be accompanied by high winds, heavy rains, quickening darkness, change in barometric pressure, and other elements that may also induce fear. Two opposing theories (both of which in my view are wrong) trace thunderphobia to problems in the hearing of certain dogs. One theory suggests that dogs with below-average hearing live for the most part in a comfortable, silent world that is suddenly broken into by the booming sound of thunder. The other theory claims that dogs with particularly acute hearing are more likely to be the victims. Neither of these ideas has ever actually been tested. It is more probable, at least in the case of thunderphobia, that the dog is responding to a whole cluster of stimuli, including noise, change in barometric temperature, or even the fearful response of his owner.

Unfortunately, noise phobia can be easily generalized. Many a dog starts out with a simple fear of thunder that soon progresses to fear of fireworks, vacuum cleaners, and other loud noises. This seems too obvious to state, but I will do so anyway: A mild fear is much easier to extinguish than full-blown terror.

- **Inherited shyness or "global fears."** These can be inherited traits and can be seen even in dogs who were raised, socialized, and handled correctly. Back in 1944, a researcher named F.C. Thorne investigated a whole line of 43 shy Basset Hounds descended from a single shy female. Whole strains of Basset Hounds and Beagles are afflicted with the problem. Researchers are not agreed as to whether it is dominant or recessive (or of polygenetic origin), but they do know that the trait is passed along from parent to offspring.

Breed Predilection and Genetics

There is a shy gene, explained below, and it seems that this gene is more common in some breeds than in others.

- **Sheepherding breeds.** Research indicates that sheepherding breeds are more inclined to fearfulness than other groups, and that German Shepherd Dogs (which to some extent are still

A dog in pain of any kind can suddenly become shy if he's trying to avoid human contact.

sheepherders) are more fearful than Boxers, say, or cattle dogs. However, good breeders are weeding out shy tendencies in German Shepherds. M. B. Willis, a researcher and show breeder, estimates that while about 20 percent of show German Shepherds exhibited excessive nervousness during the 1950s and 1960s, that number is down to about 2 percent today. It also seems to be true that German Shepherds of German lines are less likely to exhibit this temperament fault than are dogs from British or American lines.

Basset Hounds (and Beagles) are especially prone to inherited shyness.

It is not an accident that breeds whose main job was to be out in the unprotected open, like herding dogs, are more commonly afflicted with thunderphobia than "indoor breeds." The most commonly affected breed is the Border Collie. Scientific studies have shown that at least 50 percent of the breed is affected, with 10 percent so severely traumatized that they can injure themselves or others. Australian Shepherds are also frequent victims of noise phobias and for the same reasons.

Interestingly, different breeds express fear differently. Years ago, back in the 1950s, studies showed that when frightened, Beagles freeze and terriers run around frantically.

- **The shy gene.** There is a shy gene, although the method of inheritance is unclear. Some authorities believe that it is largely inherited from the dam; others think that it's a recessive trait. This is hard to test for because the mother models behavior for her puppies. Even if they aren't naturally shy and have not inherited a shyness gene, they can become shy just by being around her. (It is also inherited in human beings, apparently.)

Environmental Factors

Well, noise phobias are basically all about the environment, are they not? If your dog were deaf or lived in a soundproof room, he wouldn't have the problem.

- **Trauma.** A single traumatic experience occurring at about the eight-week mark in puppies can produce profound aversive effects that can last for years. On the other hand, bad experiences at 5

Herding dogs like Border Collies are particularly afflicted with thunderphobia because their main job was to work in the unprotected outdoors.

weeks or earlier seem to be quickly forgotten, and those occurring after 12 weeks can be overcome by positive training.

- **Kenneling and lack of socialization.** Studies show that dogs who have been kept in restrictive kennel conditions from birth to beyond 12 weeks of age are much more prone to fearful reactions. Dogs who have never been properly socialized or brought into contact with the outside world can develop a fear of open places and strange people. The critical window is between three and eight weeks of age. Dogs not exposed to normal stimuli during this time are more likely to become fearful as adults. Dogs left unsocialized until the age of 16 weeks have almost no chance of developing normal self-confidence. One study examined dogs from various sources and found that pet store puppies were most likely to develop social fears.

What to Do

Some kinds of shyness respond very well to therapy; in other, genetically based cases, your job is a lot more difficult.

1. **Take note(s).** Assess the level and kind of shyness/phobia. Keep a journal for a couple of weeks, noting times, places, and specific circumstances associated with the behavior. If you need to take your dog to a trainer or veterinarian, she will require this information. What precisely does your dog seem to fear? Video-record the behavior if possible.
2. **Socialize, socialize.** For dogs who are fearful of people and places, take baby steps. Reward all positive, confident behavior with a treat or encouraging caress. This means that every time your dog takes a confident step—such as approaching you or a stranger—reward him for his

confidence.

While a naturally shy dog may not ever be an outgoing extrovert, his behavior will improve over time.

3. **Provide white noise or music therapy.** If your dog has a specific phobia, such as thunderphobia, try providing some anxiety-reducing white noise, like from a television, CD, radio, or even a fan. Or try singing to your dog. Some studies have shown that the same kind of music that sends fussy babies to sleep calms animals in thunderstorms. Indeed, special tunes have been developed to replicate a beating heart and are available for sale. Harp music is supposed to be especially soothing—something to do with the vibrations of the strings. The right kind of music, of course, not only has a calming effect but also serves as a white noise that masks the sound of the storm.

4. **Desensitize him.** While fear responses of all kinds can be genetically programmed and in some cases further shaped by selective breeding, dogs possess the ability to habituate themselves to strange but harmless sounds, sights, smells, and tastes. Puppies and younger dogs (as well as some dogs on anti-anxiety drugs) may respond well to a technique called flooding, in which the fear-producing sounds are presented frequently and at full strength, often for eight hours or more. (If you can stand a vacuum cleaner running for eight hours, more power to you, that's all I can say.) Older dogs, whose fear responses are typically more intense than in puppies, appreciate a more gradual approach. For these dogs, flooding can make their fears and anxieties much worse. They respond better to gradual desensitization, in which the stimulus is presented briefly or at a low (non–fear-inducing) level. In most cases, professional help is called for to make this work.

In any case, for animals to continue to be habituated, they must be exposed to a certain level of the fear-provoking sound or sight periodically and safely. This is not a one-shot deal. This is how older gundogs are taught not to be frightened of a gunshot. (Puppies are often just subjected to the flooding and habituate themselves to the sound without any fuss.) Desensitization is done in staged trials, beginning at a very low intensity—the so-called "safe" level, which does not evoke a fearful response. If your dog fears men (not uncommon in rescued dogs), for example, you can start by introducing men to him at a distance. Reward him for even the slightest improvement in confidence (easier breathing, relaxing, and so forth). If you can extinguish the fear at a distance, you can gradually (and the key is gradually) have men approach closer and closer, rewarding the dog for a positive reaction, until eventually he loses his fear. For the quickest resolution of the problem, you should practice several times a day.

THE EXPERT SAYS

According to Peggy Swager, well-known trainer, behaviorist consultant, and author of *Training the Hard to Train Dog*, "The younger you begin socializing a shy dog, the more success you will have. And you can't stop with puppyhood. Shy dogs will need to be strongly socialized until they are at least one and sometimes up to three years old."

For thunderphobia, you can try desensitizing your dog by using recordings of thunderstorms. You can actually buy storm recordings—or if you are feeling adventurous, you can make your own. The plan sounds good but works only if the recording is good enough to fool your dog into thinking that a real thunderstorm is about to break open over his head. In reality, most dogs are smarter than that and can tell a CD from the genuine article. It is really impossible to re-create the whole thunderstorm experience, if you will. You may get the noise right, but how about the barometric changes, the darkening skies, the smell of the ozone, and the like? All of these may play into your dog's fears. You'll know if your dog is fooled by the way he initially acts upon hearing the manufactured sound. If you get a phobic response, he is indeed tricked. If he just walks away into the kitchen looking for food, you know you've wasted your time or money.

If, indeed, your dog thinks that the CD is a real storm, you can begin the therapy by playing it at a very low, non-threatening volume for five to ten seconds. At the same time, play a familiar favorite game with your dog or work on simple obedience exercises like *sit*. (See Chapter 4: Training Basics.) Use plenty of treats. Then, turn off the recording and withdraw the treats and affection. Repeat about ten times per session; as the sessions progress, lengthen the time of the recording and its volume, always watching your dog carefully to see that he remains within his comfort zone. The idea is very simple: Get the dog to associate pleasant activities with the sound of thunder. Gradually raise the level of the noise. One drawback to this whole procedure—assuming that it will work at all—is that you must initiate the process during the non-thunderstorm season (i.e., winter). The reason is that if your dog is exposed to a full-blown thunderstorm while undergoing the desensitization procedure, he will rapidly regress to his former state. If desensitization works, it usually works only to the specific stimulus (i.e., storm sounds) to which you're trying to get your dog accustomed. Your dog may not generalize the therapy and may still continue to be fearful of other loud noises.

5. **Drag out the anti-storm gear.** There is a theory that storm phobia has less to do with loud crashing noises than with the electromagnetic radiation that is formed by lightning strikes. You can shield your dog from these waves by covering his crate in aluminum foil. If he hides under the bed for comfort, stick some

For thunderphobia, try desensitizing your dog by using recordings of thunderstorms.

Lavishly praise your dog for all non-fearful behavior.

sheets of aluminum foil between the mattress and the box spring. There's even a cape on the market that covers the dog and reportedly has the same effect.

Another product fits like a tight T-shirt and provides all-over calming pressure to reduce anxiety. This really works, just like a hug. There are a bunch of theories why this is so, but no one really knows. You can also use elastic bandages to get the same result, called body-wrapping. Or you can just calmly hold your dog.

6. **Countercondition him.** By this, I mean simply add a reward to improve behavior during the fear episode. Offer to play an indoor game of fetch or tug-of-war. If not completely bonkers with fear, your dog may accept a treat from you or even from the feared object (such as "strange man"). Counterconditioning works best when done along with desensitization. If your dog is afraid of fireworks or other loud noises, buy a practice CD of the sound that you play while having your dog sit. Reward him for not reacting. If you are successful, slowly turn the volume up. As long as your dog remains calm, offer a treat.

7. **Be upbeat.** Be cheerful and happy during your dog's fear event, showing him that there is nothing to fear. Now, you shouldn't go overboard and get too gooey and empathetic. That will only serve to convince him that something really is wrong. However, you can quietly soothe and comfort him in a cheerful way. This is a natural thing to do, and contrary to what some people think, does not automatically reinforce fears in your dog. Lavishly praise your dog for all non-fearful behavior.

8. **Try hormonal remedies.** One well-tested naturally based hormone therapy is melatonin (N-acetyl-5-methoxytryptamine), an over-the-counter, natural hormone used to treat insomnia in human beings. Melatonin is thought to aid the regulation of the circadian rhythm (the 24-hour

cycle) of various bodily functions and processes. In dogs, it reduces stress without, apparently, causing drowsiness. I have known hunters who use melatonin to help gun-shy dogs get over their fears.

Melatonin is sold in both capsule and tablet form at health food stores. The usual dose for average-sized dogs is 3 milligrams. Dogs weighing more than 100 pounds (45 kg) may require as much as 6 milligrams, while dogs under 30 pounds (15 kg) should receive only 1.5 milligrams. Very tiny dogs can be given even less. Consult your veterinarian for dosage recommendations for your particular dog.

Side effects are very rare, but this substance should not be given to dogs on corticosteroids or oxidase inhibitors. Melatonin is not regulated by any federal agency, and its quality can vary from manufacturer to manufacturer. Be sure that you buy a product that contains only melatonin and is not mixed with herbs or other materials that might be dangerous for your dog. Give your dog a dose in the morning of a day when thunderstorms are predicted.

In 2007, Italian researchers experimented with chewable L-theanine tablets (sold under various brand names), an amino acid, in a blind study on phobic dogs. L-theanine produces a relaxing effect, lowing blood pressure and improving learning ability. Dogs were divided into groups, with some animals receiving the drug therapy, some getting behavioral therapy, and some receiving neither. After two months, owners using the medication reported that dogs on the tablets were significantly less fearful than the dogs of owners who used behavior modification alone.

9. **Try an herbal remedy.** Valerian is an herb that may induce muscle relaxation. However, used with other medications, valerian can cause side effects, so discuss with your veterinarian before use.

10. **Use pheromones.** You can try using a dog-appeasing pheromone (DAP) marketed in diffusers, collars, and sprays, or even simple lavender oil in a spritzer or diffuser. The jury is still out on their effectiveness. Still, they don't hurt anything, and maybe they will make you feel better. That alone is helpful to your dog.

An herbal remedy, like valerian, may help induce muscle relaxation.

IF ALL ELSE FAILS

If all else fails, try pharmacology. Several anti-anxiety medications can help with noise phobia. Your vet may prescribe anxiety-reducing drugs (serotonergics, or to a lesser extent, benzodiazepines) that target specific receptors in the brain. You and your vet may need to work together to find the medication that's right for your dog. Very effective are clomipramine and the similar amitriptyline. Both of these are tricyclic antidepressants, and both come in inexpensive generic forms. (These drugs should not be given to animals with seizure disorders.) Other choices include buspirone, a medication that enhances serotonin, and selegiline, a monoamine oxidase inhibitor (MAOI).

You may need to use these drugs for a few weeks before noticing any effects, and the dosage may have to be adjusted. For the best results from this protocol, thunderphobic dogs must take anti-anxiety medications throughout the entire storm season.

I should note that alprazolam and diazepam are classed as benzodiazepines, and prolonged use can cause addiction. However, for intermittent use, they have no par, and they work within 20 minutes. I use diazepam with my storm-phobic dog Clovis; at the first rumble (or if storms are predicted), I pop him a dose and he's good to go. Without it, he's a nervous wreck. The beauty of this medication is that it needs to be used only during the actual storm as opposed to continually, as with other anti-anxiety medications.

All pharmacological treatments should be combined with behavioral therapy, especially desensitization. As the dog improves, the drug dosage can often be reduced by 25 percent a week. When the dog has completed drug therapy successfully, he should continue to experience the stimulus occasionally so that the process of desensitization can be completed. If the stimulus is removed completely, he may regress.

What Not to Do

The worst mistake you can probably make is assuming that a shy dog will blossom into a fearless extrovert; this seldom happens, although good treatment can improve his behavior. However, the following mistakes will make things worse. Don't:

1. **Punish your dog for showing fear.** Any further unpleasant experience during a phobic episode will further convince the dog that he was right to be afraid. Dogs associate punishment with the punisher, not with the behavior.
2. **Protect him.** Don't encourage or reinforce your dog's shy behavior by picking him up and "protecting" him. This only reinforces his fear that something is actually wrong. Instead, simply be positive and encouraging.
3. **Drag or force him to experience new people, places, or activities.** This will only frighten your dog further.
4. **Chain, confine, or tie up your dog.** This kind of restriction can frighten a dog so badly that he will injure himself.
5. **Force your dog to experience the stimulus.** While the "throw 'em off the dock and let 'em swim" mentality may be tempting, such an approach only deepens and solidifies the fear in dogs, especially older ones.
6. **Depend on debatable "remedies."** Some owners are partial to homeopathic products. Homepathic remedies are not herbal remedies, which can actually work. The basic theory behind homeopathy is that if you take a tiny bit of a substance that produces the same effect as the offending stimulus and keep diluting it more and more while shaking the vial it's in, it will produce healing energies. In other words, in homeopathy, the more you dilute a remedy

Never drag your dog to experience new people, places, or activities, as this will only frighten him further.

the stronger it is, a principle not found anywhere else. One popular homeopathic remedy is Phosphorous (PHUS 30C), which is available in health food stores. Directions say to drop three to five pellets down the back of the dog's throat every 15 minutes until you start to see results. You can resume if the dog starts to get agitated again. Another homeopathic anti-storm remedy is Aconitum Napellus 30C, administered in the same manner.

Many people also swear by flower essences such as Rescue Remedy, Calming Essence, or Five Flower Formula. Or you can try a single essence like Mimulus, Rock Rose, Aspen, or Star of Bethlehem. (Star of Bethlehem is a very pretty flower but in its natural state is poisonous.) These flower essences were all developed in the 1930s by Edward Bach, a homeopathic physician. To administer, place a few drops of the remedy in water, then add to food or insert between the dog's lip and gum line. These essences are supposed to eventually cure your dog completely of his fears.

Now that I've told you what the classic homeopathic remedies are, I can tell you that no homeopathic remedy has ever been shown to work in an objective, double-blind, peer-reviewed test. However, they don't do any harm either, so if you think that they make your dog feel better, go ahead and use them. In the same way, there is no scientific evidence whatsoever to back up the claim that flower essences have any effect on your dog's emotional state, although because a lot of these remedies are pickled in brandy, you might take a swig yourself during a particularly scary storm.

7. **Breed your dog.** There is a fallacy wandering around that breeding a shy bitch will "settle her." It won't. It will just pass on the shy gene to her offspring.

TRAINING CHECKLIST

✓ Use desensitizing and counterconditioning methods.
✓ Create a positive example by staying calm and upbeat.
✓ Use herbal, hormonal, pheromone, or pharmaceutical remedies if needed to keep your dog calm and happy.

Chapter 21

Vocalization (Excessive)

Your dog is barking, howling, or yodeling all night and all day. Sometimes he seems to be doing all three at once. The neighbors are complaining.

More Than Meets the Ear

It sounds simple enough, but there's more to a bark than meets the ear. A bark is technically defined as a short, abrupt burst of canine sound meeting various scientific parameters of tonality, noise, pitch, volume, and amplitude. Technically, the bark is a cross between a whine and a howl. While a very clever noise for dogs to invent, it sounds fairly awful to people when continued for more than a few seconds. Between 13 and 35 percent of behavior complaints by dog owners concern what is termed "nuisance barking." (When Russian researcher Dmitri Belyaev started to produce tamer foxes for the fur trade, he found that along with more manageable behavior, the foxes also started barking like dogs.)

In case you haven't noticed, dogs can make a lot of noise. Researchers have discovered that dogs can make 10 separate vocalizations, through which they can convey 39 different meanings. The most famous of these noises is the bark, a sound used in defense, play, greetings, mate calling, attention seeking, warning, and more. Sometimes dogs just bark for joy!

While most dog owners firmly believe that a bark gives an intentional "message," some researchers dispute the idea. Kathryn Lord, a doctoral student in evolutionary biology at the University of Massachusetts in Amherst, postulated an alternative. Lord and others maintain in the journal *Behavioral Processes*: "The domestic dog does not have an intentional message in mind, such as, 'I want to play' or 'The house is on fire.'" Lord and her colleagues believe that barking is the auditory signal associated with an evolved behavior known as mobbing, a cooperative anti-predator response usually initiated by one individual who notices an approaching intruder. A dog barks because he feels an internal conflict an urge to run plus a strong urge to stand his ground. (The bark, using this definition, is not limited to dogs.) When the group joins in, the barks intimidate the intruder, who often flees. This finding seems contrary to the experience of most of us ordinary folks, who are quite sure that not only are our dogs are giving us a message, but that they know what it is. But there's science for you.

However, different kinds of conflict may trigger different kinds of barks. So even though your dog may not be intentionally giving you a message, you can decode the sound anyway. To the average person, it seems abundantly clear that dogs bark for many reasons, or to be more scientific about it, due to several kinds of conflict. They may be seeking attention, alerting their owners to an intruder, communicating with other dogs, defending their territory, or expressing their emotions: joy, fear, boredom, and so on. Some dogs, especially of the herding breeds, may bark when anything is moving, especially if it is moving and making noise at the same time. Your vacuum cleaner is a perfect example.

So who is right? Do dogs intentionally send messages through their barking or not? My bet? Sometimes. That's usually safe enough. What is not in dispute is that noisemaking is a natural behavior that has actually been encouraged by breeding over the centuries. Dogs have been bred to bark at intruders, bark for treats, and vocalize while hunting game. It's only comparatively recently, as urban populations increased, that dog noises were labeled irritating and their owner evicted.

Dog noises are often contagious; when one dog barks, the rest join in, even if they have no clue as to what is going on. The fancy name for this is "allelomimetic barking" (or howling). It just means copycat, which in itself is a weird term to apply to dogs and may be the reason why scientists prefer to say allelomimetic. Howling is especially allelomimetic, especially when initiated by the lead wolf or dog.

For most of us, a sharp bark once in a while is a neutral event. Don't expect to eliminate barking completely, any more than you would want to train your child not to laugh or cry. It is a natural behavior, and some breeds tend to bark more than others. But when barking continues for many minutes (or even, it seems, hours) nerves get frayed, and not just yours. The entire neighborhood is a victim. (After all, your neighbors do not care if your dog is well housetrained or chews your walls. That's your problem. Barking, on the other hand, is everyone's headache.) And just as important, a dog who barks that much is not a happy dog; to a certainty, he is lonely or bored.

A dog barks because he feels an internal conflict—an urge to run plus a strong urge to stand his ground.

Causes

Barking probably has more "causes" behind it than any other single behavior; let's look at some of them.

Medical Conditions

Dogs with medical problems manifest them in all sorts of vocal ways, including barking, howling, whining, moaning, and even growling.

- **Canine cognitive dysfunction (CCD).**
  Older dogs can suffer from canine cognitive

dysfunction, a condition similar to Alzheimer's disease in humans, in which they may not even be aware that they are barking, or if so, why. A dog with CCD can bark at nothing and for no reason, literally for hours.

- **Sickness or chronic pain.** Some dogs also howl or bark when they are not feeling well. If this is a new behavior for your dog, check it out.
- **Obsessive-compulsive behavior.** While uncommon, an obsessive compulsive behavior can manifest itself in excessive vocalizing. Dogs with this disorder may bark at minor, inappropriate things—like a falling leaf.

Wolf Heritage

The howl of a large dog is acoustically indistinguishable from that of a wolf. The fundamental "howling" lies between 150 and 780 Hz and includes up to 12 harmonically related overtones. Although wolves are noted for their signature howl, they actually whimper, yelp, moan, and bark more often than they howl. (It is sometimes said that wolves don't bark, but they do, just not as frequently as dogs do.) The wolf bark is lower pitched and less variable in its structure than dog barks are. Wolves bark mainly as a warning, while dogs bark for innumerable other reasons. Mature wolves bark much less frequently than juveniles, and it is this juvenile barking that breeders have selected for in

Some dogs howl or bark when they are not feeling well.

developing watchdogs. (Dog behavior is closely patterned after that of juvenile wolves.)

Wolves often bark for the following reasons:

- **Mark territory.** Making noise shows the other wolves exactly where their territory is. In fact, wolves have learned to howl in harmony, making it seem as if there are more wolves present than there really are.
- **Attract mates.** Like many animals, wolves "call" for their mates.
- **Communicate with pack members.** Wolves vocalize to communicate with their pack members while hunting. Interestingly, wolf pups never howl—they bark like dogs. Adults howl to locate each other (especially during storms, it seems). Not surprisingly, perhaps, wolves from different geographical locations howl differently. The pitch may actually change direction four or five times.

Breed Predilection and Genetics

Not all breeds are equal in the vocalization department. The following are particular candidates for the noisemakers' hall of fame:

- **Excitable breeds.** Dogs who bark a lot tend to be more excitable in general than those who don't. Such breeds include Miniature Schnauzers, Cairn Terriers, West Highland White Terriers, Pomeranians, Chihuahuas, and Scottish Terriers. In fact, almost all terriers, including the tiny Yorkshire, tend to bark a whole lot.
- **Small herding breeds.** Although most herding dogs are quiet enough, the Shetland Sheepdog, smaller than most other herders, uses his bark rather than his body to get the attention of the sheep. Therefore, he is a barker. Sheep guardians, on the other hand, tend to bark only when something is really wrong—so as not to alarm the sheep unnecessarily.

- **Some game-trailers.** Certain scenthounds are encouraged to be vocal when chasing game, like Foxhounds, who tend to be vocal even when there are no foxes anywhere in sight. Beagles, bred to trail game, are also barkers. Other game trailers, like Bloodhounds, run silently. (They're supposed to follow human beings and not give themselves away.)
- **Coonhounds.** These extremely vocal breeds are also EXTREMELY LOUD. In coonhunting trials, they actually get points for the loudness of their vocalizations.
- **Pack hunting dogs.** Pack hunting dogs, like Beagles and Basset Hounds, commonly make three sorts of sounds: the bark, the howl, and the bay. The bark is similar to an ordinary dog's bark, while the howl is a haunting, mournful melody used the same way a wolf howls and for most of the same reasons. Howling dogs often sound sad, but get a group of hounds or huskies together and they will often howl apparently for the sheer pleasure of hearing themselves sing. The bay is a kind of cross between a howl and bark and is typically triggered by the sight or smell of a prey animal. This is the noise the dog makes on the hunt, which signals to the hunter that game is indeed afoot.
- **Watchdogs.** Some watchdogs, including the German Shepherd Dog, Australian Shepherd, Akita, Rottweiler, and Doberman Pinscher, have the enviable reputation of being excellent watchdogs without becoming nuisance barkers.
- **Basenjis.** Basenjis don't bark readily (the larynx is not shaped in such a way as to easily allow it), although he can summon up an unnerving set of vocalizations that may make you wish he would stop doing whatever it is he's doing and just bark like the Yorkie down the street. The Basenji will bark only under extreme provocation and then emit only a bark or two. The Basenji noise, compared to a regular bark, conveys little information as to where it originated, thus confounding the leopards who usually prey upon them in their native Africa.
- **New Guinea Singing Dog.** The New Guinea Singing Dog, another primitive breed, makes a noise like a rooster that can be heard for miles (km) in the mountainous ranges of his homeland.

Environmental Factors

Although I'm listing these behaviors separately, they often occur at the same time. Confined dogs, for example, are often lonely dogs too.

- **Warning.** Your dog is doing you a favor, even though he may be mistaken about whom or what constitutes a danger. (Technically, a warning bark is an example of a hair-trigger agency detector, or alternately, a hyperactive agent detection device. Take your pick. All dogs are equipped with this early warning detection system, and we should be thankful for it.)

- **Confinement.** Dogs are wanderers by nature, and many respond to being crated by setting up a session of barking until they are let out.
- **Attention-seeking behavior.** Dogs can learn to bark to achieve desired results, such as food or attention.
- **Boredom.** Dogs do bark to entertain themselves. If you are wondering why they don't get tired of barking, it seems that it bothers them as little as talking all the time bothers the talker—although both dog and human can become hoarse.
- **Environment distractions.** Do you live in an exciting neighborhood? While some dogs bark because they are bored, others bark because they are overexcited and overstimulated.
- **Multiple dogs.** If you own multiple dogs, the chances are greatly increased for nuisance barking. Not only are you increasing the chances that at least one is a barker, but one barker vastly increases the odds that the others will start barking as well.
- **Indecisiveness.** As mentioned earlier, a bark can signal conflicting impulses. Run or fight? Maybe just bark. It seems to be a tension reliever.
- **Separation anxiety.** Separation anxiety is a leading cause of barking. In this case, the problem to be solved is not the barking but the separation anxiety that leads up to it. If your dog barks mainly when he is left alone, and especially if his barking is accompanied by house soiling or destructive behavior, please see Chapter 19: Separation Anxiety.

The New Guinea Singing Dog makes a noise like a rooster that can be heard at long distances.

What to Do

Take comfort in the fact that when you curb excessive barking, you are not denying your dog the pleasure (or to you, the benefit) of some, particularly alert, barking. The object is to reduce the noise to a manageable level.

1. **Take note(s).** Assess the level and kind of barking. Try to determine if the

Dogs who can follow basic obedience commands are easier to train out of excessive vocalizing than are those who can't.

barking is secondary to another problem, such as separation anxiety or fear of loud noises. In the latter case, the primary problem must be dealt with first. Keep a journal for a week or two, noting times, places, and specific circumstances associated with the behavior. If you need to take your dog to a trainer or veterinarian, she will need this information. Video-record the behavior if possible.

2. **Consult your vet.** In some cases, your dog may have canine cognitive dysfunction or a similar medical reason for barking.

3. **Be patient.** Changing this behavior takes time. If you get angry, you will only upset your dog and encourage more barking.

4. **Reward your dog.** When your dog is calm, relaxed, and quiet, reward him—and ignore him when he isn't. The first step in controlling this undesirable behavior is to get a handle on why your dog is barking in the first place. Praise him and give him plenty of attention when he is not barking—for attention seekers, that's all the reward they need.

5. **Get your dog into obedience training.** Obedient dogs, who come when they are called and sit on command, are easier to train out of excessive vocalizing than are those who aren't trained. If your dog is completely untrained in other respects, sign him up for obedience classes. If he is trained, teach him to lie down when a barking situation arises. (See Chapter 4: Training Basics.)

6. **Neuter your dog.** Unneutered dogs, both males and female, vocalize more than their neutered counterparts.

7. **Teach him to bark on cue.** For certain barkers, especially dogs who are triggered to bark when something moves, this tactic works. Keep some treats on hand. When the dog starts barking, say "Quiet!" If he stops barking, even momentarily, give him a treat. But do not treat him when he is barking—ever.

8. **Give him something else to do.** The fancy name for this is "response substitution." Teach your dog a different way to react to stimuli, and it's your job to make sure that he succeeds. The goal is to teach your dog alternate ways to get your attention. Such methods include tail wagging or looking to you for a response. For example, if your dog barks at the vacuum cleaner, practice having him sit-stay. This is called "sit and watch." If he remains quiet, walk up and give him a treat. One friend of mine taught her dog to run upstairs whenever the doorbell rang. Continue this

strategy, but over time make the treat giving intermittent. Gradually, your dog will learn to accept the vacuum cleaner as part of the family.

9. **Desensitize your dog to noise stimuli.** Owners appreciate a quick warning bark when visitors arrive, but dogs who continue to bark become irritating very fast. So your aim should be to allow such a quick notice—but no more. You can teach this with the help of a friend who will agree to be the door knocker. The knocking should be very quiet. (There is usually a relationship between the loudness of the stimulus and the response.) When he barks once or twice only, say "Enough"—and as soon as he stops, give him a pet or quick treat. Always use the same "stop" word. Then distract him and reward no further barks. Repeat about ten times each session.

10. **Make your dog feel secure.** The cause of fear barking is obvious—the dog feels threatened. This is a particularly dangerous problem for dogs kept on chains; they feel vulnerable, and a vulnerable dog is much more likely to bite. Never try to reassure a fear barker—that is a reward for the behavior. It's best to act calm, chipper, and happy. If you have a puppy, make sure that he meets a lot of different people in different situations. Later, the appearance of unusual things should elicit a quick "alert" bark but no prolonged fear barking.

Never try to reassure a fear barker—that is a reward for the behavior. It's best to act calm, chipper, and happy.

11. **Exercise your dog.** Well-exercised dogs are tired dogs. Tired dogs bark less because they have less energy to spend on vocalizing. Fact.

12. **Bring your dog indoors.** If your dog is an outdoor barker, bring him inside when he starts to bark. Dogs are social creatures, and yours may simply be bored and lonely. Whatever he was barking at is out sight once he's brought in. Your dog is also safer indoors—less apt to escape the property or be teased by kids, for example.

13. **Limit his horizons.** Dogs who bark incessantly at every passerby (even though they themselves are in the house) may quiet down if the triggering environmental stimuli are removed—such as preventing the dog from seeing the mail carrier through the window. You can keep him inside the house with the blinds drawn, for example. If your dog is spending a lot of time outdoors, he may be overstimulated by the goings on and should be brought in the house.

14. **Rearrange the furniture.** If your dog

Never inadvertently reward a barking dog by encouraging him, yelling at him, or talking to him while he's engaged in the behavior.

is indoors and barks out at the neighborhood, he's probably standing on the back of the couch staring at the street. Make this impossible.

15. **Try a shaker can.** For some noisy dogs, the sound of a shaker can (filled with coins or something similarly noisy) interrupts the barking pattern and attracts the dog's attention. At that point, praise him. You might need to keep several cans around the house. This kind of interruption works much better than yelling because your dog won't associate it directly with you.

What Not to Do

You will never completely silence a vocal dog, but some mistaken tactics will make the problem worse. Don't:

1. **Encourage your barker.** Many people unintentionally encourage a barking dog. For instance, when someone is at the door, they say "Look! Someone's here! Who is it?" in an excited voice. The excitement in your voice is contagious, and the dog will join in. Owners may even feed or pet a barking dog, which the dog cleverly assumes is some kind of reward for his behavior. Practice a deadpan response to doorbells and knocking, and your dog will follow suit. If he continues to bark, don't speak soothingly to him—that will also encourage his behavior.

2. **Yell and shout at the barker.** Never reward barking. And believe it or not, yelling and screaming is a kind of reward because it is attention, and dogs bark to get attention. If you allow him to bark for a long time and finally break down by yelling at him, you've only taught him that if he barks long enough, he'll achieve his goal. Even if the dog correctly interprets your yelling as a "punishment," his response will more likely be to fear you than to stop barking.

3. **Touch or talk to your dog.** On the same note, gently speaking and touching a barking dog can inadvertently reinforce his behavior.

WHEN ALL ELSE FAILS

When all else fails, try a citronella collar. The citronella collar, a fairly benign type of "remote punishment," works by automatically emitting a citrus-like scent when the dog barks. The scent is vaguely pleasant to people, but dogs hate it. It has the further advantage of lingering in the air—so when you come home, you'll know whether or not the dog was barking in your absence. Research shows that citronella collars are more effective than the traditional and painful shock collar. A downside of this collar is that extreme care must be taken in adjusting it. A poorly adjusted citronella collar can pick up the sound of other dogs barking and unjustly release a puff of the hated smell into the wearer's innocent face. All kinds of correction collars also have the same defect—they can't reward the dog positively when he doesn't bark.

4. **Tie up your dog.** A tied-up dog has lost one of his major options in the face of danger or uncertainty: fleeing the situation. His inner conflict makes him bark.
5. **Shock your dog.** In general, I strongly discourage the use of most "corrective" or "shock" collars. These collars are designed to emit an electrical "stimulation" (i.e., shock). Research shows that most of them don't work, especially for long-time established barkers; they are also cruel in that they attempt to suppress a natural behavior. In some cases, they can turn a gentle dog into an aggressive one. With fear barkers, such collars only make them more fearful.

TRAINING CHECKLIST

✓ Reward your dog when he is quiet.
✓ Give a barking dog an alternative behavior.
✓ Make sure that your dog gets plenty of exercise and time with you.
✓ Bring an outdoor barker in the house.
✓ Desensitize your dog to noise stimuli.

Chapter 22

Walking Woes

Walking problems occur in a variety of guises: Dogs lag, tug, or bite at the leash. They lunge at other dogs, wildlife, or strangers. This is natural behavior. It's up to you to teach your dog something that is completely foreign to him.

Some dogs will lag or tug on the leash, which makes walking them much more difficult than it has to be.

Causes

Dogs are generally fairly accommodating about performing this rather unnatural function. If they don't cooperate, it's usually not too difficult to figure out why.

Medical Conditions

Certain neurological and other medical disorders can cause problems in dogs walking on a leash, but it's unlikely, especially in the case of a puller. If you suspect something medical is wrong, talk to your vet. Most of the time, however, the problem is behavioral.

Wolf Heritage

Wolves don't walk well on leashes. They can be trained to do it, but they won't heel. So we can safely say that your dog's wolf heritage makes him naturally resistant to being pulled along on a leash. However, he does have a natural inclination to follow, so wise owners take advantage of this natural feature in their dog's makeup. Being a strong leader—that is, becoming someone your dog *wants* to follow—will make the whole process much, much easier.

Breed Predilection and Genetics

Walking problems occur mostly in independent breeds. Some of these dogs forge ahead, some insist on going where they please (or nowhere at all), and some just lie down if they don't feel like walking. Here are representative breeds of each of these types:

- Siberian Huskies
- Chow Chows
- Basset Hounds

Environmental Factors

- **Improper training techniques.** Yanking on the leash, yelling at your dog, and other misguided attempts to force your dog to "listen" will backfire.
- **The wrong equipment (or the right equipment used incorrectly).** Different dogs respond differently to different walking aids. Some dogs walk better with a harness, others with a head halter. These must be used properly in conjunction with proper training practices. A device that is wrong for your dog or used incorrectly will just make the problem worse.
- **Outside distractions.** Distractions, like other dogs, fascinating squirrels, and strange-looking people across the street, can all conspire to complicate your task.

THE EXPERT SAYS

According to dog handler Jean Di Fatta, "Dogs pull on the leash because they are rewarded for doing so. When you let them stop, forge ahead, or turn suddenly to check out a bug, they are getting a reward for pulling. You are inadvertently reinforcing their behavior. You can make it easy for your dog to make the right decision by never giving in to his desire to strain on the lead. Always use a wide (and preferably padded) collar when working with a stubborn dog. You don't want him to get his way, but you don't want to hurt him in the process."

What to Do

Teaching your dog to walk well will make your life (and your dog's life) much easier. Taking a well-trained dog for a walk is one of life's greatest quiet pleasures. And you meet interesting people too!

1. **Make walking fun.** My first advice is to make at least part of the walk both fun and exercise intensive for your dog. Let him stop and smell and look around. At least part of the time, slacken the lead and let him make a few decisions. You can let your dog know that it's okay to "do his own thing" using a clear command like "Free time!" to let him know that he is temporarily "off the hook," even though he's still on the leash. Give him a long enough lead so that you can verbally call him back to your side before he reaches the end of the leash and feels physical pressure.
2. **Use the correct leash and collar.** Sometimes all you need to do is to change the walking

Some dogs walk better with a traditional collar and leash, while others prefer a harness.

equipment and your problem is solved. Let's start with the leash. Your best bet is a 6-foot (2-m) leather leash; it is the easiest on the hands of all materials. Fabric leashes can create friction burns, while chain leashes are heavy, noisy, and breakable. Retractable leashes are usually a poor idea; they don't give you enough control, and dogs end up wrapping them around trees or worse. In fact, retractable leashes can produce problems for some people, as they are hard to handle and bulky. However, if you're comfortable with them, there is no reason not to use them.

Harnesses other than the front-loop harness are also poor choices. These devices go around the dog's strongest part. They were designed for cart and sled dogs, and most dogs lean into them and start pulling automatically. Only tiny dogs with fragile necks should wear them, and even these dogs do better with a front-loop harness. If you do use a conventional collar, keep it high up on the neck, as far above the shoulders as possible; this is the weakest part of the neck and hence the part that affords you the most control. A buckle collar should be all that you need.

3. **Try a head halter or front-loop harness.** These are wonderful for children and elderly owners to use. The head halter and front-loop harness not only give you more ultimate control of the dog but also prevent the oppositional reflex (pulling) instinct from taking over. While some dogs hate the head halter, some owners have noticed that the gentle pressure on the nose loop and behind the head has a soothing effect. My favorite, however, is the front-loop harness, which dogs seem to instinctively like (no training period necessary, either) and which is not only completely safe but allows your dog to sniff around.

4. **Get in some pre-walk exercise.** To help control an exuberant dog, give him a chance to run off some of that extra energy in the yard (if you have one) before the actual walk. You can try a few games of fetch or flying disk. If you don't have a yard, some indoor games like tug may help.

5. **Start off calmly.** If you get all excited at the prospect of a walk, so will your dog. So if the problem is that your dog is hyper and out of control, dial it back. Be low-key and nonchalant, and your dog will take his cue from you. (This takes some practice, of course.) Make him sit before you

walk out the door. And it should be you, not the dog, who decides when it is time to leave the house.

6. **Keep walking.** While in training mode, your job is to lead. Do not allow your dog to sniff, eliminate, or stare at passersby. You are in control. Keep walking at a good clip. Until your dog is completely trained, consider walks a training session. You may have to find alternate ways of exercising your dog until he becomes reliably leash trained, as training sessions of all kinds have to be kept relatively short.

7. **Reward him when he walks correctly.** Use food as a reward, a soft, easily swallowable high-value treat that your dog doesn't get at other times. Cheese is a natural, and so are hot dogs, cut into peanut-sized cubes. Walk along with the treat enclosed in your left hand or waist pouch, right at his nose level. A food-oriented dog will become so fixated on your hand that he won't dream

SMART STUFF

If your dog chews his leash, consider a chain leash, or even better, spray his regular leash with a dog-repellent.

Make your dog's walks more fun by allowing him to stop and wander at times and just enjoy the scenery.

Walk or jog your dog every day, if he's fit for it, for a good exercise regimen.

of going anywhere. Every few steps, treat him. When he stops pulling, gradually increase the number of steps you take before rewarding him.

8. **Become an oak tree.** Do not walk forward as long as there is tension on the lead. If your dog pulls, come to a dead stop and wait. Do not move until he stops pulling. When your dog looks back at you to see what the heck is the matter, praise him for his attention. The point is to let him know that you aren't going anywhere until he stops pulling.

9. **Walk away.** This is an alternate tactic to the oak tree. When your dog pulls, start walking in the opposite direction, or if he continues to pull, keep changing directions. This keeps him moving but indicates to him that he needs to go where you go.

10. **Walk (or jog) your dog every day.** The more you practice, the better. It is not enough to let your dog "self-exercise" in the backyard, no matter how spacious it is. Most dogs simply won't do it. Dogs have a need for directed walks.

11. **Teach your dog the *look at me* command.** (See Chapter 4: Training Basics.) This will help keep his attention focused during those difficult times.

12. **Add a pack.** Lots of working and high-energy breeds actually do better if you place a dog pack on their backs. It gives them something to think about other than lunging forward, and it tends to slow them down.

What Not to Do

Your goal is to make this walking business fun. Don't do anything that gets in the way of this important goal, like:

1. **Let the dog walk ahead of you.** Your dog needs to look to you for leadership and to show him where to go. Don't get into the habit of letting him take the lead. Actually, dogs are usually more relaxed as followers.

2. **Punish your dog.** Punishing your dog will only make him want to get away from you. That is exactly the opposite of the behavior you wish to encourage.

3. **Use harsh collar corrections.** Never jerk on the leash if your dog isn't walking to your satisfaction—especially with tiny dogs, puppies, or fragile dogs. Don't pull on the collar as a correction either; that sets up an oppositional reflex, and your dog will pull pack.

TRAINING CHECKLIST

✓ Make walking fun.

✓ Be the leader.

✓ Consider food bribes.

✓ Use the best collar and leash for *your* dog.

✓ Teach the *look at me* command. (See Chapter 4: Training Basics.)

Resources

Breed Clubs

American Kennel Club (AKC)
8051 Arco Corporate Drive, Suite 100
Raleigh, NC 27617-3390
Telephone: (919) 233-9767
Fax: (919) 233-3627
E-Mail: info@akc.org
www.akc.org

Canadian Kennel Club (CKC)
200 Ronson Drive, Suite 400
Etobicoke, Ontario M9W 5Z9
Telephone: (416) 675-5511
Fax: (416) 675-6506
E-Mail: information@ckc.ca
www.ckc.ca

Fédération Cynologique Internationale (FCI)
Secretariat General de la FCI
Place Albert 1er, 13
B − 6530 Thuin
Belgique
www.fci.be

The Kennel Club
1-5 Clarges Street, Piccadilly, London W1J 8AB
Telephone: 0844 463 3980
Fax: 020 7518 1028
www.the-kennel-club.org.uk

United Kennel Club (UKC)
100 E. Kilgore Road
Kalamazoo, MI 49002-5584
Telephone: (269) 343-9020
Fax: (269) 343-7037
www.ukcdogs.com

Pet Sitters

National Association of Professional Pet Sitters (NAPPS)
15000 Commerce Parkway, Suite C
Mt. Laurel, New Jersey 08054
Telephone: (856) 439-0324
Fax: (856) 439-0525
E-Mail: napps@petsitters.org
www.petsitters.org

Pet Sitters International
201 East King Street
King, NC 27021-9161
Telephone: (336) 983-9222
Fax: (336) 983-5266
E-Mail: info@petsit.com
www.petsit.com

Rescue Organizations and Animal Welfare Groups

American Humane Association (AHA)
63 Inverness Drive East
Englewood, CO 80112
Telephone: (303) 792-5333
Fax: (303) 792-5333
www.americanhumane.org

American Society for the Prevention of Cruelty to Animals (ASPCA)
424 E. 92nd Street
New York, NY 10128-6804
Telephone: (212) 876-7700
www.aspca.org

Royal Society for the Prevention of Cruelty to Animals (RSPCA)
RSPCA Enquiries Service
Wilberforce Way, Southwater,
Horsham, West Sussex RH13 9RS
United Kingdom
www.rspca.org.uk

Sports

International Agility Link (IAL)
85 Blackwall Road
Chuwar Qld 4306, Australia
Telephone: 61 (07) 3202 2361
Email: steve@agilityclick.com
North American Dog Agility Council (NADAC)
P.O. Box 1206
Colbert, OK 74733
Email: info@nadac.com
www.nadac.com

North American Flyball Association (NAFA)
1333 West Devon Avenue, #512
Chicago, IL 60660
Telephone: (800) 318-6312
Email: flyball@flyball.org
www.flyball.org

United States Dog Agility Association (USDAA)
P. O. Box 850955
Richardson, TX 75085-0955
Telephone: (972) 487-2200
Fax: (972) 231-9700
www.usdaa.com

The World Canine Freestyle Organization, Inc.
P.O. Box 350122
Brooklyn, NY 11235
Telephone: (718) 332-8336
Fax: (718) 646-2686
E-Mail: WCFODOGS@aol.com
www.worldcaninefreestyle.org

Therapy

Delta Society
875 124th Ave, NE, Suite 101
Bellevue, WA 98005
Telephone: (425) 679-5500
Fax: (425) 679-5539
E-Mail: info@DeltaSociety.org
www.deltasociety.org

Therapy Dogs Inc.
P.O. Box 20227
Cheyenne WY 82003
Telephone: (877) 843-7364
Fax: (307) 638-2079
E-Mail: therapydogsinc@qwestoffice.net
www.therapydogs.com

Therapy Dogs International (TDI)
88 Bartley Road
Flanders, NJ 07836
Telephone: (973) 252-9800
Fax: (973) 252-7171
E-Mail: tdi@gti.net
www.tdi-dog.org

Training

American College of Veterinary Behaviorists (ACVB)
College of Veterinary Medicine, 4474 TAMU
Texas A&M University
College Station, Texas 77843-4474
www.dacvb.org

American Kennel Club Canine Health Foundation
P. O. Box 900061
Raleigh, NC 27675
Telephone: (888) 682-9696
Fax: (919) 334-4011
www.akcchf.org

Association of Pet Dog Trainers (APDT)
101 North Main Street, Suite 610
Greenville, SC 29601
Telephone: (800) PET-DOGS
Fax: (864) 331-0767
E-Mail: information@apdt.com
www.apdt.com

International Association of Animal Behavior Consultants (IAABC)
565 Callery Road
Cranberry Township, PA 16066
Telephone: (484) 843-1091
E-Mail: info@iaabc.org
www.iaabc.org

National Association of Dog Obedience Instructors (NADOI)
P. O. Box 1439
Socorro, NM 87801
Telephone: (505) 850-5957
www.nadoi.org
Veterinary and Health Resources

Academy of Veterinary Homeopathy (AVH)
P. O. Box 232282
Leucadia, CA 92023-2282
Telephone: (866) 652-1590
Fax: (866) 652-1590
www.theavh.org

American Academy of Veterinary Acupuncture (AAVA)
P.O. Box 1058
Glastonbury, CT 06033
Telephone: (860) 632-9911
Fax: (860) 659-8772
www.aava.org

American Animal Hospital Association (AAHA)
12575 W. Bayaud Ave.
Lakewood, CO 80228
Telephone: (303) 986-2800
Fax: (303) 986-1700
E-Mail: info@aahanet.org
www.aahanet.org

American College of Veterinary Internal Medicine (ACVIM)
1997 Wadsworth Blvd., Suite A
Lakewood, CO 80214-5293
Telephone: (800) 245-9081
Fax: (303) 231-0880
Email: ACVIM@ACVIM.org
www.acvim.org

American College of Veterinary Ophthalmologists (ACVO)
P.O. Box 1311
Meridian, ID 83860
Telephone: (208) 466-7624
Fax: (208) 466-7693
E-Mail: office11@acvo.com
www.acvo.com

American Heartworm Society (AHS)
P. O. Box 8266
Wilmington, DE 19803-8266
Email: info@heartwormsociety.org
www.heartwormsociety.org

American Holistic Veterinary Medical Association (AHVMA)
P. O. Box 630
Abingdon, MD 21009-0630
Telephone: (410) 569-0795
Fax: (410) 569-2346
E-Mail: office@ahvma.org
www.ahvma.org

American Veterinary Medical Association (AVMA)
1931 North Meacham Road, Suite 100
Schaumburg, IL 60173-4360
Telephone: (800) 248-2862
Fax: (847) 925-1329
E-Mail: avmainfo@avma.org
www.avma.org

ASPCA Animal Poison Control Center
Telephone: (888) 426-4435
www.aspca.org

British Veterinary Association (BVA)
7 Mansfield Street
London
W1G 9NQ
Telephone: 0207 636 6541
Fax: 0207 908 6349
E-Mail: bvahq@bva.co.uk
www.bva.co.uk

Canine Eye Registration Foundation (CERF)
VMDB/CERF
1717 Philo Road
Urbana, IL 61803-3007
Telephone: (217) 693-4800
Fax: (217) 693-4801
E-Mail: CERF@vmdb.org
www.vmdb.org

Orthopedic Foundation for Animals (OFA)
2300 E. Nifong Boulevard

Columbia, MO 65201-3806
Telephone: (573) 442-0418
Fax: (573) 875-5073
Email: ofa@offa.org
www.offa.org

US Food and Drug Administration Center for Veterinary Medicine (CVM)
7519 Standish Place
HFV-12
Rockville, MD 20855-0001
Telephone: (240) 276-9300 or (888) INFO-FDA
Email: AskCVM@fda.hhs.gov
www.fda.gov/cvm

Publications
Books

Anderson, Teoti. *The Super Simple Guide to Housetraining.* Neptune City: TFH Publications, 2004.

King, Trish. *Parenting Your Dog.* Neptune City: TFH Publications, 2004.

Libby, *Tracy. High-Energy Dogs.* Neptune City: TFH Publications, 2010.

Swager, Peggy. *Training the Hard-to-Train Dog.* TFH Publications, 2009.

Yin, Sophia. *How to Behave so Your Dog Behaves.* Neptune City: TFH Publications, 2004.

Magazines

AKC Family Dog
American Kennel Club
260 Madison Avenue
New York, NY 10016
Telephone: (800) 490-5675
E-Mail: familydog@akc.org
www.akc.org/pubs/familydog

AKC Gazette
American Kennel Club
260 Madison Avenue
New York, NY 10016
Telephone: (800) 533-7323
E-Mail: gazette@akc.org
www.akc.org/pubs/gazette

Websites

Nylabone
www.nylabone.com

TFH Publications, Inc.
www.tfh.com

Index

Note: **Boldfaced** numbers indicate illustrations.

cat chasing, 107–108, **108**
causes of problem behaviors, 9–11. *See also specific behavioral problem*
Cavalier King Charles Spaniels, 127
CCD. *See* canine cognitive disorder
CDH2 gene (compulsive behavior), 194
chaining, 63, 74, 222
chasing behavior
    breed predilection, 103–105, **103**
    causes, 102–105
    environmental factors, 105–106
    medical conditions, 102
    overview, 101, **102**
    predatory behavior vs., 106
    what not to do, 108–109
    what to do, 106–108
    wolf heritage, 102
checkups, veterinarian, 130
chewing behavior. *See also* separation anxiety
    breed predilection, 113, **114**
    causes, 112–113
    environmental factors, 114–115
    medical conditions, 112–113
    overview, 111–112, **112**
    what not to do, 119
    what to do, 115–118
    wolf heritage, 113
Chihuahuas, 113
children
    snapping breeds and, 60, **60**
    supervision of, **64**, 65
chocolate, 123
Chow Chows, 239
citronella collars, 235
Clark, Andy, 18
coat, breeds with heavy coats, 135, **136**
Cocker spaniels, 127
collars
    citronella, 235
    Elizabethan, 198
    selection of, 239–240, **240**
    shock, 235
    ultrasonic, 199
    wireless, 146, 147
Come command, 43–44, **44**
commands, 42–48, **42–46**, 147, 232, 242

commitment to relationship, 13, **14**, 40
competition, **80**, 81–82
competitive behavior, 83–84
competitive games, 75
compulsive disorders, 126, 134, 173. *See also* obsessive-compulsive disorder
containment or confinement, 145–146, **159**, 222, 231
Coonhounds, 230
Coppinger, Raymond, 32
coprophagia, 122, 124, 130
Coren, Stanley, 16
counterconditioning, 72, 180–181, 206, 219
coyote roller, 146
crating, 119, **145**, 146, 161, 208, **208**
crowding, 84–85, **84**
cutoff signals, 58

D

Dachshunds, 113, 127
DAP (Dog Appeasing Pheromone), 104, 208, 220
dead animals, eating, 124–125
decompression areas, 146
Delise, Karen, 74
demodectic mange, 192
dental disease, 193
depression, 56
desensitizing
    aggression, 72, 88
    fearfulness, 217–218
    noise stimuli, 233
    separation anxiety, 206–207
dewclaws, 194
Di Fatta, Jean, 239
Diamond, Kathy, 115
diarrhea-producing illnesses, 152
diet. *See also* toxic or harmful foods
    allergies, 152
    carbohydrates in, 126
    changes in, 71, 157, **158**
    deficiency in, 113
    low-protein, 169
    malnutrition, 56, 95
    nutritious foods, 130
dietary indiscretions. *See also* feeding
    breed predilection, 127

causes, 126, **126**
environmental factors, 128–129
medical conditions, 126–127
overview, 121–125, **122**, **124**
what not to do, 131
what to do, 129–130
wolf heritage, 126–127
digging behavior
    breed predilection, 134–135
    causes, 134–137
    medical conditions, 134
    overview, 133–134
    what not to do, 139
    what to do, 137–138
    wolf heritage, 134
diseases. *See* health issues
Doberman Pinschers, 195
dock diving activity, 167
Dodman, Nicholas, 27, 96
Dog Appeasing Pheromone (DAP), 104, 208, 220
dog bites, 14, 53. *See also* aggression
dog doors, 158, 159, **159**
Dog Genome Project, 32
dog walkers, 157–158, **207**, 209, 243
doggy day care, 157–158
doggy doorbell, 158
dog-proofing, 117
dog-to-dog aggression
    breed predilection, 82–84
    causes of, 79–85
    dealing with, 85–90
    dominance hierarchy, 77–78, **78**
    environmental factors, 84–85
    what not to do, 90–91
    wolf heritage, 79–82
dog-to-dog jealously, 182, **182**
domestication of dogs, 24–26, 32
dominance aggression, 53–54, 59
dominance hierarchy, 77–78, **78**
dominance structure, 79–81
dominance-based corrections, 73–74
down command, 44–45
dragging dogs, 222, **222**
drooling, 96
drug therapies, 72–73
dry skin, 192

Dedication

For everyone who works in pet rescue.

About the Author

Diane Morgan is a freelance writer specializing in dogs and Eastern spiritual traditions. She is a five-time winner of the Dog Writers Association of America (DWAA) Maxwell Award for excellence in dog writing and lives in Vero Beach, Florida, with her husband and family (including several dogs).

Photo Credits

Alice Mary Herden Green-Fly Media LLC (Shutterstock.com): 107, 120, 193
Al_Kan (Shutterstock.com): 57
Morten Normann Almeland (Shutterstock.com): 172
Almotional (Shutterstock.com): 42
AnetaPics (Shutterstock.com): 10, 85, 143, 144, 165
Utekhina Anna (Shutterstock.com): 229
Anneka (Shutterstock.com): 222
ARENA Creative (Shutterstock.com): 205
argo74 (Shutterstock.com): 168
Art_man (Shutterstock.com): 52
AVAVA (Shutterstock.com): 40, 98
Darren Baker (Shutterstock.com): 184
marilyn barbone (Shutterstock.com): 220
Joe Belanger (Shutterstock.com): 159
Peter Betts (Shutterstock.com): 100
Bine (Shutterstock.com): 65
bitt24 (Shutterstock.com): 72
Blessings (Shutterstock.com): 17
Olga Bogatyrenko (Shutterstock.com): 157
Rob Bouwman (Shutterstock.com): 181
Jeroen van den Broek (Shutterstock.com): Cover Photo
Penny Brooks (Shutterstock.com): 59
Joy Brown (Shutterstock.com): 62, 129, 182, 210
Rob Byron (Shutterstock.com): 233
Caimacanul (Shutterstock.com): 15
Gina Callaway (Shutterstock.com): 55, 90, 176
Carolina (Shutterstock.com): 215
Roberto Cerruti (Shutterstock.com): 31
kevin, Chen(Shutterstock.com): 135
Costin Cojocaru (Shutterstock.com): 240
David Dalla Costa (Shutterstock.com): 122
Cynoclub (Shutterstock.com): 24, 80

Jeff Dalton (Shutterstock.com): 39
Phil Date (Shutterstock.com): 73
Peter Dean (Shutterstock.com): 105
Melanie DeFazio (Shutterstock.com): 50
Mo Devlin: 33
Dogboxstudio (Shutterstock.com): 228
Nick Doronin (Shutterstock.com): 204
Dushenina (Shutterstock.com): 9
Shchipkova Elena (Shutterstock.com): 241
Eponaleah (Shutterstock.com): 6
Andrey Eremin (Shutterstock.com): 116
Fnsy (Shutterstock.com): 63
Four Oaks (Shutterstock.com): 82
Marcie Fowler - Shining Hope Images (Shutterstock.com): 66
Jose Gil (Shutterstock.com): 242
Godrick (Shutterstock.com): 67
Warren Goldswain (Shutterstock.com): 3
Gontar (Shutterstock.com): 112
Ilya D. Gridnev (Shutterstock.com): 125
Miroslav Halama (Shutterstock.com): 162
Hamik (Shutterstock.com): 70
Hannamariah (Shutterstock.com): 236
Mat Hayward (Shutterstock.com): 124
Iofoto (Shutterstock.com): 117
Petar Ivanov Ishmiriev (Shutterstock.com): 140
Eric Isselee (Shutterstock.com): 30, 35, 47, 106, 128, 206, 212
Jagodka (Shutterstock.com): 34
Joop Snijder Photography (Shutterstock.com): 216
Alister G Jupp (Shutterstock.com): 76
Anne Kitzman (Shutterstock.com): 198
KristinaShu (Shutterstock.com): 196
Geoffrey Kuchera (Shutterstock.com): 22
Holly Kuchera (Shutterstock.com): 14
Jesse Kunerth (Shutterstock.com): 188

Artem Kursin (Shutterstock.com): 108
Kzenon (Shutterstock.com): 25, 64, 232
Bianca Lagalla (Shutterstock.com): 145
A. Laengauer (Shutterstock.com): 224
Reinhold Leitner (Shutterstock.com): 171, 177
Leungchopan (Shutterstock.com): 7
Dr. Alan Lipkin (Shutterstock.com): 114
Mona Makela (Shutterstock.com): 219
Steve Mann (Shutterstock.com): 84
Marafona (Shutterstock.com): 218
MCarper (Shutterstock.com): 160
Sue McDonald (Shutterstock.com): 20, 170
Richard A. McGuirk (Shutterstock.com): 207
Andrzej Mielcarek (Shutterstock.com): 227
Mikeledray (Shutterstock.com): 97
Dudarev Mikhail (Shutterstock.com): 27
Mikola (Shutterstock.com): 202
Lipowski Milan (Shutterstock.com): 21
Neeila (Shutterstock.com): 117
Suzi Nelson (Shutterstock.com): 150
Piotr Niecicki (Shutterstock.com): 49
Oliveromg (Shutterstock.com): 12, 41
Siamionau pavel (Shutterstock.com): 48
Steve Pepple (Shutterstock.com): 60, 130
Zacarias Pereira da Mata (Shutterstock.com): 4
Michael Pettigrew (Shutterstock.com): 92, 214
Anastasija Popova (Shutterstock.com): 79
Pressmaster (Shutterstock.com): 36
Prodakszyn (Shutterstock.com): 89
Ratikova (Shuttestock.com): 136
Raywoo (Shutterstock.com): 78
Mary Rice (Shutterstock.com): 234
Robynrg (Shutterstock.com): 126
Pavel Sazonov (Shutterstock.com): 154

Sbolotova (Shutterstock.com): 18
Scorpp (Shutterstock.com): 158
SueC (Shutterstock.com): 110
Susan Schmitz (Shutterstock.com): 87, 95, 197
John S. Sfondilias (Shutterstock.com): 190
Annette Shaff (Shutterstock.com): 44
Shutterstock.com: 28, 54, 83, 142, 187, 195, 238
E. Spek (Shutterstock.com): 153
Rob Stark (Shutterstock.com): 94
Alexey Stiop (Shutterstock.com): 146, 200
Katsai Tatiana (Shutterstock.com): 103
Barna Tanko (Shutterstock.com): 178
Vitaly Titov & Maria Sidelnikova (Shutterstock.com): 139
Tstockphoto (Shutterstock.com): 118
Suponev Vladimir (Shutterstock.com): 86
Svetlana Valoueva (Shutterstock.com): 43
Petr Vaclavek (Shutterstock.com): 53
Kachalkina Veronika (Shutterstock.com): 102
Visceralimage (Shutterstock.com): 148
Vnlit (Shutterstock.com): 46
Edward Westmacott (Shutterstock.com): 132
WilleeCole (Shutterstock.com): 152, 164, 192, 208
Wjarek (Shutterstock.com): 156
Yellowj (Shutterstock.com): 174
Lisa F. Young (Shutterstock.com): 38
Ryhor M Zasinets (Shutterstock.com): 231

All other photos courtesy of Isabelle Francais and TFH archives.

Nylabone®

Safe, Healthy Chewing
Since 1955